Stories of Indian
Gods and Heroes

Attention Authors

Manas Publications is fighting a war to tell the world that India can win the battle not only by the bullet but also by pen. We are converting fighters into writers. There is no dearth of intellectuals in our country, however, their knowledge is confined to them only. No sincere effort has been made by any other publisher to channelise their knowledge, that is why the talent of every intellectual remains latent. An author always presents the raw material in the shape of a manuscript and it is the job of the publisher to convert it into a finished product. Manas has been continually motivating intellectuals and publishing their manuscripts for more than two decades and would like to publish your manuscript too. If you or your colleagues have a manuscript ready for publication or are working on it, contact us with a detailed synopsis and list of contents. Manas can also suggest you a suitable title for writing related to your area of expertise. Manas is known for its publishing quality. We take utmost care in publishing and also give wide publicity to the book and its author through our national and international distribution network.

Stories of Indian
Gods and Heroes

WD Monro

With sixteen Illustrations by
Evelyn Paul

Manas Publications
(We Convert Fighters into Writers)
New Delhi-110 002 (INDIA)

MANAS PUBLICATIONS
(Publishers, Library Suppliers, Importers & Exporters)
4402/5-A, Ansari Road (Opp. HDFC Bank)
Darya Ganj, New Delhi-110 002 (INDIA)
Off. © 23260783, 23265523, Res. © 23842660
Fax: 011-23272766
E-mail: manaspublications@vsnl.com
manaspublications@yahoo.com

2011

ISBN 978-81-7049-407-2
Rs **795**.

Printed in India at
RK Print Services, Delhi
and published by Mrs Suman Lata for
Manas Publications, 4402/5-A, Ansari Road
(Opp. HDFC Bank),
Darya Ganj, New Delhi-110 002 (INDIA)

Preface

THE word "Preface" suggests to many youthful minds something learned and dry, and the result is that the Preface is not read. Certainly a book of stories like these ought not to be burdened with anything dry at the outset; but if the stories themselves are to prove reasonably interesting, it will do no one any harm to know something about the books in which they are found and the people among whom the books were written.

The language in which these tales have come down to us is called *Sanskrit*, a name which has nothing to do with that of any people—like the names English, French, German, etc.—but is simply an adjective of which our term "high class," though not an exact translation, gives a good idea; because Sanskrit was the language spoken by the Brahmans, —*i.e.* the priests—and kings of various different nations of ancient India, while other classes of society commonly spoke what was called *Prákrit*, a vulgar form of Sanskrit.

Many centuries before the time of Christ, there came into India a people who called themselves

Áryas, which means simply "nobles." From this name we derive the word "Aryan," denoting races belonging to the same great family, which includes, besides these invaders of India, many Western races, as may be easily seen by comparing Greek and Latin, and most modern languages of Europe, with the ancient Sanskrit.

The Aryan invasion of India doubtless covered many years, or even centuries; but it seems reasonable to think of 1500 B.C. as an average date for their settlement and earliest writings. From that time, they spread over the whole of Northern India, but made far less impression upon the South. The languages of Southern India are markedly different from those of the North; all the latter—excepting those of Mongolian or Muhammedan origin—bear the most evident tokens of close relationship to Sanskrit; and some words are used to this day in Northern India exactly as they appear in the most ancient Hindu Scriptures, not less than 3,000 years old.

These first Hindu Scriptures take the form of hymns, of which a large number were, sooner or later, gathered together in collections known as *Vedas*. Of these there are four, though one of them is clearly altogether later than the others, and is much less respected. The most famous of all is the *Rig-Veda*, a collection of rather over a thousand hymns. These are addressed to gods who bear a strong resemblance to the gods of the Norsemen—the distant cousins, so to speak, of these old Aryans, and who are nothing more nor less than the great forces of Nature personified. Fire and water, sky and sun, thunder and rain: all these and many lesser natural phenomena were worshipped under one name or another. And these hymns, as may be imagined, are full of every sort of myth and fancy drawn from the various manifestations of God in Nature.

As time goes on, we find, on the one hand, attempts to discover some foundation underlying this simple Nature-worship, to ask deeper questions on the problems of religion; and, on the other, new stories about the old gods, and new gods coming to join the ranks of the others, all with a strong tendency to exaggeration and to many things resembling and, unhappily, far surpassing in impropriety the grosser features of the Greek mythology.

While none of our stories are drawn wholly from the Veda, some of the characters mentioned in this book appear more or less frequently in the hymns. Vasishtha and Viswamitra are supposed to have written some of them; traces of the Urvasi myth appear; and many of the gods of whom we shall hear are mentioned, though the position they occupied in Vedic days changed, in many cases, as time went on.

Passing over a large mass of important literature attached to the Vedas—though some of it contains a great deal of matter similar to that from which our tales are drawn—we should notice next the great Epics of India, the *Ramayana* and the *Mahabharata*. The former deals with the South of India, the latter with the North. The word Ramayana simply means "Story of Rama," a great hero, who is represented as the seventh of the incarnations of the god Vishnu. This deity, according to Hindu legend, had appeared several times on earth already, generally in forms not human: for example, a fish, a tortoise, a boar, etc. This Vishnu, under one name or another, is, perhaps, the most popular of all the Hindu gods. Under the name of Rama, he still receives the worship of millions; and Krishna, the incarnation following Rama, is even more popular than his predecessor, though, according to Western notions, very much less worthy of honour.

The Ramayana is a poem of great length—about 60,000 lines—but it is short compared with the Mahabharata. This enormous poem—evidently the work of many hands, at widely differing dates—runs to no less than 210,000 lines as long as those of Macaulay's *Armada.* The main subject is the struggle between two branches of a royal family for supremacy in the country round Delhi; but every part of the poem abounds in "side shows" of every sort, and there are few well-known subjects or legends of Hindu religion which are not handled in the Mahabharata.

The main story of each of these great poems is shortly told in this book; and several of the minor tales are taken, either wholly or in part, from one or the other.

The last important class of books which gives us material for these tales is called the *Puranas.* These are, generally speaking, much later than the Epics, and some of them clearly belong to a date comparatively recent. The main idea of the

Puranas is definitely religious, and most of them are written to glorify some god in particular. They generally begin with an account of the origin of the world, and go on to describe the various appearances and achievements of the god. The scope which this arrangement gives for stories of every kind is practically unbounded.

If we turn now to consider very briefly some of the most remarkable points about this great literature, the first thing to which I would draw attention is *the vast period* which it covers. We are fairly safe in carrying the limits of "classical" Sanskrit as late as about 1,000 A.D.—a very rough estimate, no doubt—and we thus see that, beginning with the Vedas, the whole covers a period of no less than 2,500 years. The Sanskrit of the Veda differs from that of the Epics much as the language of Homer differs from that of Sophocles; but we still have a period of something like 2,000 years during which the language has continued to put forth books great and small with less alteration in the style and vocabulary than has taken place during the last three centuries in Britain. This is due mainly, no doubt, to the fact that Sanskrit was a sacred language, and occupied, among the various kingdoms of India, a place similar to that taken by Latin during the Middle Ages in Europe.

Considering the enormous time which the literature had for its development, three further points strike us as remarkable.

In the first place, all the works from which these tales are taken, and the great majority of Sanskrit writings in general, are either properly *religious* or, at any rate, saturated with religious ideas. Gods and demons, prayers and sacrifices, appear everywhere. This is not without parallel, to some extent, in Western literatures; but in these the religious element, without being suppressed, has come to be only one of many branches of writing, generally within the course of a few centuries from the birth of any given literature.

Secondly, it is astonishing to find in a literature of such antiquity and extent as that of India, an almost entire lack of anything worthy of the name of *history*. A foundation of historical truth, doubtless, underlies both the Ramayana and the Mahabharata, and, possibly, parts of some Puranas. There is, again, a poem called the *Rajatarangini*, which relates, in poetry, the history of the kings of Kashmere at a certain epoch. But the great Epics and the Rajatarangini are, at best, a very poor and distant equivalent for that solid work of historical prose which has played so great a part in every important Western literature and in that of Muhammedan kingdoms as well. That little or nothing of the kind appears in the best twenty-five centuries of Sanskrit literature is a phenomenon truly extraordinary. Hundreds of racy and interesting stories may be culled from Persian and Arabic historical works; and it is deeply to be regretted that, from its many centuries and its vast opportunities of observation, ancient Hindu literature has left us no similar sources of instruction and entertainment.

It would not be fair to pass from the subject without some notice of a feature of Hindu literature which is the less attractive because so peculiarly characteristic. *Exaggeration* holds a place in these writings altogether without parallel in any literature of similar extent. For thousands and tens of thousands, the old Hindus wrote millions and billions, or millions of billions; and the dimensions of mountains, rivers, beasts, birds, fiends, etc., etc., are described in terms which are not merely absurd but often too wild to be even amusing. It must also be admitted that along with this rather wearisome feature one finds, in the records of Hindu gods and heroes, many things that are unpleasant and disgusting, not merely to ourselves, but to cultivated and even common-place Hindus: dark spots which only show the darker for the gaudy setting of fantastic miracles in which they are generally framed. For this book we have naturally chosen only the brightest and best, and the tendency to exaggeration has been moderated as far as possible, though to omit everything would be to disfigure the original beyond recognition and to present a picture of ancient Indian life quite remote from the truth.

I confess, for my part, that I find in the Wonderland of Hinduism no hero half as interesting as Odysseus, in the West, or Rustem, in the East. But, when all is said and done, I hope my readers will find among the heroes and heroines of these stories some who are worthy of their interest and not wanting in the best elements of dignity and courage.

W. D. M.

Contents

Illustrations

Stories of Indian Gods & Heroes

Chapter I

THE TALE OF VISWAMITRA

OF old there lived a king named Gadhi, to whom was born a son named Viswamitra. Father and son naturally both belonged to the Kshatriya caste, the second of the four great Hindu castes, consisting of warriors and kings. But it so happened that the child Viswamitra was born with an instinctive longing to become a Brahman, that is, a member of the priestly caste, the highest of all.

Now it is a well-understood doctrine of the Hindu scriptures that a man born in a certain caste can in no wise pass from that caste to a higher one during his lifetime. Such a passage can, it is written, only come through a man's being born again, after death, into the higher caste, after having lived a full life in the lower scale. But Viswamitra's desire was that even in the one lifetime he should enjoy the triumph of overcoming the strict rule and fierce opposition of the priests, and rise to their level by the practice of great austerities.

This ambition did not consume his heart in earlier years. In truth, it was not till his life—a life of thousands of years—was far advanced that certain happenings kindled to a flame this spark of longing for a Brahman's powers. But when the flame was once roused, it burned in him with all-consuming fierceness. Long and dread were the austerities which he underwent, and vehement the ardour of those who sought to baffle his purpose; but in the end he won his way to the goal.

When Viswamitra succeeded to his father's kingdom, it chanced on a time that he assembled a great army and set forth to make a kingly progress through the land. In the course of this he came to the hermitage of Vasishtha, a sage of great renown and sanctity. Viswamitra, as a monarch of his fame deserved, was received with much honour and cordiality by the hermit and the Brahmans who shared his forest retreat. At first Vasishtha set before the king only the simple fare of which he and his fellow-ascetics daily partook; and Viswamitra, who felt himself as much honoured by the hospitality of the sages as they were by his visit, accepted the fruits and herbs with all contentment. Sage and monarch then held amiable converse for a while; but, as Viswamitra's visit drew to its end, Vasishtha declared his wish to entertain the king and his army in a manner befitting royalty. Viswamitra declared himself sufficiently honoured by being admitted to the hospitality of so famous a sage; but his host pressed the entertainment upon him, and in the end

Viswamitra accepted the favour cheerfully, as well he might.

Besides wonderful powers gained by his austerities, the sage Vasishtha possessed a marvellous cow, Sabala by name. This was none other than the Cow of Plenty, who could bring forth, at her master's wish, endless supply of whatever he required, whether it were a simple meal or a mighty army.

Forthwith, then, at her lord's behest, Sabala provided for the delighted guests hills of rice, lakes of broth, and cakes, honey, and all manner of viands and drinks in lavish abundance. From Viswamitra himself to the least of his retainers, all alike were bounteously supplied with the choicest that they could desire.

The monarch meditated with amazement and delight upon the wondrous powers of the hermit's cow; and keen desire to own her filled his breast.

"Jewels," he cried to the saint, "are the portion of kings; this cow is a jewel, therefore let her be mine! For her I will give a hundred thousand kine!"

But Vasishtha replied, courteously yet firmly, "Not for ten million kine would I part with her, O monarch. She is my friend and guardian; from her comes all my supply of both mind and body—yea, my very life I owe to her. The feast that was spread before thy host was due to her bounty. For these and many other reasons, I never can part with Sabala."

Then Viswamitra, full of eagerness, renewed his petition with offers of vastly greater price. He spoke of thousands of elephants, dight with golden chains; thousands of well-bred, high-mettled steeds; hundreds of splendid chariots; and kine by the million.

But Vasishtha would not be tempted. He replied that it was through the cow that he gained the power and the means to perform all his sacred rites and austerities, and that she was to him as his very life. And, in truth, what was wealth, that he should barter for it her who could supply him with all he desired?

His prayers availing nought, Viswamitra determined to bear away the cow by force. Rudely seized by his men, the cow lamented sorely, thinking that her master had cast her off. Breaking from those who sought to restrain her, she fled, moaning to her lord, and poured forth her sad complaint to him. At first Vasishtha was much downcast; for he knew the might of Viswamitra, and, beholding the vast host attending the king, he told Sabala that he feared resistance to such power would be all in vain. To this the cow replied that the Brahman's might was above all, and that before his divine powers the warrior must fail and bow his haughty head.

"Thy power," she cried, "hath brought me here, such as I am; and at thy word I can bring forth those who will confound the proud monarch!"

Encouraged by these words, Vasishtha called on the cow to create a host of warriors, and thereon the cow brought forth thousands of armed men, of fierce barbaric tribes, all accoutred in the finest mail, with sword and battle-axe. But Viswamitra was possessed of many wondrous weapons, and, hurling these, he flung the host of Sabala's warriors into dismay and rout.

Then Vasishtha called on the cow again to create with all her power. Forthwith there sprang into

The Rider on the Snow-white Bull

existence legions of mountaineers and barbarians, of tribes dwelling on the borders of Hindustan and far beyond. They fell, in their myriads, with chariots, horses and elephants, on Viswamitra's army, which shrivelled and perished in a moment before that dread onslaught.

Beholding this dire overthrow with amazement and grief, the hundred sons of Viswamitra rushed fiercely on the sage. But against him their valour was of small avail; one cry he uttered, one glance he sped, and straightway they fell before him, burnt to ashes.

In woe unspeakable Viswamitra fled from the disastrous combat; and now began the long struggle in which he sought to attain to powers which would give him equality with his erstwhile host and now hated foe. He delivered his kingdom to his one surviving son, and then betook himself to the life of a hermit, hoping by dreadful austerities and mortification of the flesh to win the power of vengeance. With this intent, on the slopes of snow-crowned Himalaya, he sought by stern ascetic practice to honour the grim deity, Siva, also called Mahadeva—the Great God—who loves the Abode of Snow.

When many days had thus passed, Mahadeva, rider on the snow-white bull, appeared to him and asked what boon he would gain.

"Give me," cried Viswamitra, "the wondrous science of the bow, and command over every mystic weapon wielded by gods and demons, saints and sprites!"

His prayer was granted; and Viswamitra, triumphant in the pride of his new arms, was filled with fierce joy, as he pictured to himself the overthrow and ruin of the Brahman sage. Hastening to Vasishtha's hermitage, he launched his dreaded darts, till the saint's dwelling perished utterly in scorching flame. Men, birds, and beasts fled aghast, and brought the dismal tidings to their lord. But he, nothing daunted, cried wrathfully that Viswamitra's folly had sealed his doom, and that he should perish in his sin that very day. No whit affrighted, Viswamitra came forth to the fray, and, with scornful countenance, plied the sage with weapon after weapon so strange and dreadful that none of merely human power could stay their malice. Vasishtha, however, parrying all with his magic wand, stood unharmed and serene. Then Viswamitra, as a last resource, took that dart which bears the name of Brahma, the Creator. So awesome was this weapon, that, when the king essayed to use it, the inhabitants of heaven itself, and of the lower regions, quailed. But Vasishtha, strong in the power of mighty spells, absorbed the Brahma weapon into his person. Sparks and smoke brake forth from every pore of his skin, and his whole body glowed like the sceptre of Yama, lord of the dead.

Loud and jubilant were the praises of the sage's friends; and Viswamitra, abashed and disconsolate, confessed that before the Brahman's sanctity the warrior's might was poor and weak. But, instead of giving up the struggle, he prepared to undergo further purifying austerities, determined now that he would compass nothing less than the attainment of Brahman sainthood itself.

So he departed from his home again, he and his queen alone, and sojourned afar in the south country. There he practised penance strict for many a long day, even for a thousand years. At the end of this came Brahma, the Creator, and told him, with air benign, that these austerities had won for him the state of Rajarshi, or Kingly Sage. But Viswamitra was wroth, and answered with scorn, "All my toil has been for nought, it seems, if royal sainthood is mine only guerdon from the gods."

Pondering thus, he turned again to his task, and with sternest zeal pursued the path of austerity and penance.

About this time, it chanced that there reigned in a certain part of Hindustan a king named Trisanku. Virtuous and self-controlled, he nevertheless yielded to one overmastering passion—the desire that he might ascend to heaven in his human body. To this end he sought the aid of Vasishtha, but that sage bade him lay aside an aim so desperate. Trisanku then sought out the hundred sons of Vasishtha; for they, like their sire, were hermits of renown, and lived a life of retirement and penance in the south country. With due reverence and supplication the monarch approached them and made his petition; but they chid him sternly for cherishing the vain hope that what the illustrious father had denied the sons would or could ever grant.

Great was the wrath of Trisanku at this second rebuff. He turned from Vasishtha's sons, exclaiming fiercely, "I go to seek the aid of other sages."

Scarce had the words left his lips, when the sons of Vasishtha, in hot anger at this scornful reply, laid on him the curse that he should be turned into a Chandala, or outcast of the lowest sort. Then they turned, each one, to retirement and meditation again.

Sad indeed was the change that passed upon King Trisanku in fulfilment of the Brahmans' curse. His skin became swart in hue and rough, his hair dropped out, his ornaments turned to those of attendants at funerals, and courtiers and friends shrank and fled from him in fear and loathing. Yet, undaunted by this grievous plight, he cherished his high ambition unbroken, and now sought none other than Viswamitra for counsel.

The warrior-hermit gazed with compassion on his fellow monarch, now brought so low, and questioned him concerning his condition and hopes. Hereto Trisanku made reply: "I sought to win heaven in this my human body, and to that end I invoked the aid of my priest and his sons. But neither he nor they would grant their help; therefore, illustrious sage, I come to thee. With these pure lips, which have never known stain of falsehood, I swear by a warrior's faith that I shall abide steadfast in my purpose. Oh, aid me in my quest, for now have I no helper but thee!"

Now, Viswamitra might well be moved by this plea from one of his own order, who, like himself, was seeking high and holy privileges above the common lot of warriors. But, further, it had befallen King Trisanku to be thwarted and buffeted by those same enemies who had wrought Viswamitra so much ill. Therefore it was with much sympathy that the hermit listened to the king's tale; and mildly he replied, "Fear not, noble king! I myself will be thine aid, and all the holiest saints will I invite to the ceremony, whereby thou shalt be assured of an ascent to the skies, even in the unchanged body which thou now wearest."

Therewith Viswamitra sent forth his pupils far and wide to summon all the greatest and holiest to the rite. Among those to whom the message was sent were Vasishtha and his sons. The messengers returned in due time, announcing that all had promised to attend, save Viswamitra's hated rival and his sons, who had scornfully replied to the summons, "What heed will gods and saints pay to a sacrifice celebrated by one not born a priest? Can we—Brahmans—partake of such a sacrifice without defilement, and shall we look to such as Viswamitra for purification?"

Thus had run the answer of their angry scorn; but with equal wrath did the outraged Viswamitra retort on them a heavy curse, replying to those that brought back word, "Those base ones, who have thus scorned me, and have disallowed the claim to sacrifice which my years of penance have earned, shall sink in disgrace to a vile estate. Seven hundred times shall they be born in the condition of loathly outcasts, wearing the cast-off clothing of the dead, satisfying their hunger with the flesh of dogs. Great Vasishtha himself, proud fool, shall himself catch the stain he seeks to fix on me. As a fowler, rejoicing in the death of living creatures, shall he be born, and shall live a base existence for many a long day, unsoftened by any tender thought."

Then, turning to the other sages and pupils

assembled round him, he solemnly declared the purpose of their coming together: to wit, that through this rite Trisanku might forthwith, in his natural body, rise to heaven.

Ere, however, we pass to consider how the ceremony went, there falls to be told another tale of the manner in which the wrath of Viswamitra overtook his rival's sons. It skills not to argue which tale deserves the greater credit—some, perchance, might venture to suppose that this was a second stroke that fell on them when the first was past. In either case, the story runs thus:

Vasishtha chanced one day to meet on the road a certain king, of whose household, among others, he was the priest. The king bade him give place, but the saint replied, with due courtesy, that it was the warrior's duty to give way to the Brahman. On this the king, enraged, smote the saint with his staff; whereupon Vasishtha cursed him to become a cannibal. Viswamitra heard this curse, though unseen himself, and willed that a man-eating fiend should possess the king. Things being thus, the king passed forth, and the first man he met was Vasishtha's eldest son, Saktri, whom he straightway devoured. In course of time, all Vasishtha's sons perished in like manner. Stricken with grief, the saint sought to slay himself in divers ways. He cast himself from the top of Mount Meru; but, soft as cotton, the rocks received him unscathed. He entered a burning forest, but the flames touched him not. He cast himself, heavily weighted, into the sea, but the waves cast him ashore; and into a river, bound, but the stream loosed his bonds and delivered him alive upon the bank. Failing by these and other methods to divorce himself from life, he betook himself once more to his forest dwelling, and on the way well-nigh met the death he had so long pursued in vain. For the man-eating king met him, and would have devoured him; but Vasishtha, to save the monarch from the unpardonable guilt of devouring a Brahman saint, cast the evil spirit out of him, and restored him to his right mind, after twelve years' bearing of the curse.

Returning now to Viswamitra's sacrifice: the sage and others versed in sacred lore began the solemn rite, and, at the end of due chanting of hymns and the like, Viswamitra called on the gods to honour the offering; but the Immortals would not hear.

Then, in exceeding great wrath, Viswamitra invoked the power of his own merits, gained by penance, to enable the king to rise to heaven, despite the neglect of the gods. So potent was his invocation that, before the wondering gaze of all, Trisanku winged his way aloft towards the abodes of the blest. But not so did he escape the watch of the Immortals, and Indra cried out upon him, "Hence, Trisanku! Here is no dwelling for thee! Fall headlong, fool, to earth again!"

Thus adjured, Trisanku fell swiftly downward, but, as he fell, screamed to Viswamitra for help. Hearing him, the kingly hermit, bending all his energies to the task, stayed the fall of the monarch. Then, by mighty power gained by penance and study, Viswamitra created seven stars in the southern sky, over against the seven stars of the Northern Bear, and in the midst of these Trisanku hung the while. Borne on the tempest of his rage, the sage was fain—

so weird and vast was his power—to form new gods, who should less keenly combat his wayward purposes; but gods, Daityas and saints, alike dismayed, approached to turn him from this dread resolve. To them the haughty sage gave ear, indeed; but, changeless in his purpose, he withheld his new threats only on the agreement that Trisanku should ascend to heaven as he had desired and, by Viswamitra's help, had begun to do. To this the needed consent was given, and gods and sages had rest again; and Viswamitra, this object gained, set off to other regions in new quest of merit and might.

It will be seen that even the gods themselves were led sometimes to fear those who sought and gained superhuman powers by constant austerities and mortification of the flesh. Thus it was with them, as they noted the warrior-sage's stern continuance in the strictest forms of penance. They sought to turn him from his aim; and once, for a time, the great ascetic suffered himself to be beguiled and led into the enjoyment of pleasures which undid the merit of years of self-control. Then he came to himself with shame and self-reproach, and bent himself with ever greater sternness to the pursuit of Brahman sainthood. In vain did the celestials renew their former allurements; the saint was no longer to be tricked, and the guile recoiled on the agents themselves. Wrath burned in Viswamitra's heart as he contemplated these efforts to keep him from his goal; and this yielding to anger itself robbed him of much merit. But ever did he recover from these checks, and set himself unweariedly to the task of mastering every sense and passion.

Thus he would stand unmoved for days on one foot, with arm upstretched, feeding on nought but air. In the fiery heat of summer he would sit in the midst of four kindled fires, the sun, a fifth, blazing overhead. In the furious rain-storms of his land, both day and night, no canopy save the heavy clouds shadowed his head, while the wet grass was his only couch. Thus for another thousand years he persevered, and the gods trembled as they watched. But the sage abated his rigours not a jot. Leaving the Himalayan slopes, he journeyed eastward, and with unheard-of strictness spent a new thousand years in utter silence. With the fierceness of his penances his body became shrivelled and dry as a log of wood; but nought could bend the intention of his steadfast heart.

Then, when the thousand years were past, Viswamitra sate him down to a humble meal, when, lo, Indra in Brahman guise drew near to beg a dole. Faint and spent with hunger, Viswamitra yet uttered no word, but, silent and self-controlled, gave every crumb to him that asked. As he passed triumphant through this last bitter test, the fires of his gathered merit, as it were, blazed forth, and thick clouds of smoke rolled round his brow. Utter dismay seized the denizens of all three worlds; gods and saints, Daityas and Nagas, came in terror to the Lord of all, to beg him to stay the dire results of still withholding the boon for which Viswamitra practised such austerities.

"Against him, Lord," they cried, "nor lure nor threat prevails—his vow he keeps with unfaltering purpose. If his boon be not granted, then doubtless he will go on to practise such penance as will peril the very fabric of the Universe. Already the earth is racked with throes of anguish; gloom pervades the world below; what terrors may we not fear if Gadhi's son be driven to seek yet higher powers for the accomplishment of his purpose? Grant him, we pray thee, what he seeks, and give safety to creation!"

Thus entreated, Brahma at length, with the company of the Blest, drew near the sage and hailed him sweetly, saying:

"Hail, son of Gadhi, Brahmarshi now! For to this state of Brahman sainthood have thy ceaseless labours and penances entitled thee. Long life and peace and joy be thine; go whither thou wilt at thine own pleasure."

Then Viswamitra, full of triumph, addressed the All-father with reverence, saying, "If indeed my title to Brahmanhood be made sure, then let it be confirmed by Vedic formula, and let the sacrifice own me its master. Also, let the saint Vasishtha come and confirm the bestowal of the boon."

Then came Vasishtha, that famous hermit, and hailed his new-made peer, acknowledging his claim to Brahman saintship; and Viswamitra, in turn, pressed on his former foe the honours of hospitality with all kindness.

Thus ended the high quest of the warrior Viswamitra, for, despite the opposition of priest and god, he had won, at length, equal rights with the great hermit who of old overthrew him so utterly. But whether the friendship with which he and Vasishtha met, no the day when Brahma hailed him as Brahmarshi, endured as it began, might in any case be somewhat doubted; while, if the following tale be no less true than what has gone before, it is plain that concord between two such rivals may well be short-lived.

II

In the days after Viswamitra had gained his title to the rank of Brahman, there lived an exalted monarch named Harischandra, himself a Rajarshi, as Viswamitra also once had been. This Harischandra was a ruler of the highest parts, and in his realm men loved virtue more than evil, and sickness and calamity visited them but rarely.

It chanced on a day that King Harischandra hunted in the forest; and as he chased a deer, he heard the oft-repeated cry, "O save us!", as of women in distress. These voices proceeded—though the king could not know this—from the embodied forms of certain Sciences, which the mighty Viswamitra was bringing under his control; and they, never having been so enslaved before, cried out for deliverance.

Now, had King Harischandra acted in his own natural spirit of wisdom and self-control, he would doubtless so have proceeded in the matter that no evil came of it. But by ill chance it happened that there was present a malignant being, the Spirit of Opposition, who goes to and fro in the world, seeking to hinder all that makes for progress; and he, beholding Viswamitra obtaining the mastery over new and mighty sciences, was casting about in his mind how he might stay the sage in his endeavour, yet saw not any means to that end. "For," thought he, "this Viswamitra is glorious in power, and my might is less than his; the Sciences will forthwith be overcome unaided."

Then, hearing the king shout, "Fear not!", in answer to the cry for help, the Spirit of Opposition thought, "The difficulty is solved; I shall enter into the king, and he will do the work for me."

So the spirit entered into Harischandra; and he, burning with anger at the thought of such iniquity being wrought thus shamelessly in the by-ways of his kingdom, advanced towards the spot whence the cries came, exclaiming loudly that the wretch who thus transgressed should forthwith perish under the stroke of his royal arrows. Hearing this threatening language, the great sage was much enraged; and, coming upon him in this mood, King Harischandra was greatly confounded, and stood trembling like a leaf. Casting himself down, he cried, "Be not wroth, great lord! I sought only to do the warrior's duty, which is, according to the sacred law, to fly to the protection of those who cry for aid."

The saint deigned not to answer directly, but asked, "To whom, O king, must thou give gifts? Whom protect? And with whom wage war?"

"To Brahmans first," replied the king, "should I give gifts; the terrified I should protect; with foes should I make war."

Then said Viswamitra, "If, then, thou regardest thy duty, give me, a Brahman begging of thee, a fitting fee."

To this the king responded gladly, "Whate'er thou desirest, great sage, consider it already given, even to my kingdom, my wife, my life itself."

"Whate'er thou desirest, Great Sage" 32

On this, Viswamitra demanded such a fee as might be given for the Rajasuya sacrifice; and, being asked to speak more exactly, he demanded the surrender of all Harischandra's possessions, leaving only his person and his personal merits, with his wife and his son. With willing heart and unmoved countenance the king gave assent to the gift. Then the sage commanded that, as Harischandra's kingdom and rule had now passed into his own hands, the king should forthwith, at his behest, go forth from that country, clad in coarse bark-cloth, on foot, with wife and child alone.

Having meekly assented, the king prepared to depart, but the sage again accosted him with a demand for further fees; and though the king pleaded that nought had been left to them save their three bodies, yet Viswamitra was urgent, and threatened to curse the king if a generous fee were not forthcoming. In great straits, Harischandra pleaded for time to find money, and promised to be ready with the fee in the space of one month. This prayer Viswamitra deigned to grant, and bade the king go in peace for the time.

So Harischandra fared forth in lowly plight, with his wife and son alone. Loud was the lament of the citizens when they saw their great and good sovereign brought so low. "Alas! good master," they cried, "why dost thou leave us? Let us attend thee and be with thee, on whom we depend for all our welfare. Alack, that thy queen, unused to walking, should go thus on foot, leading her son by the hand; and thou too, before whom were wont to go out-riders on horses and elephants! What will befall thee, soiled with dust and worn with fatigue? Without thee we are as empty shadows; thou art our father, our joy, our city, our heaven; leave us not, O best of kings!"

Then King Harischandra, much moved, wavered in his going, out of pity more for the forlorn mood of his subjects than for his own sad plight. Viswamitra saw him linger, and brake forth on him angrily, saying, "Shame on thy faithless dealing, thou, who, having promised to give me thy kingdom, now desirest to withhold the gift!"

The king, trembling, murmured, "I am going." But the sage, not content with roughness of speech, raised his staff and cruelly belaboured the poor young queen as Harischandra led her away. The king's heart swelled with grief; but, "I am going," was all that he said.

Thus Harischandra, with his wife Saivya and the boy, left his country and went on foot to Benares. But Viswamitra was there before them, and sternly demanded the fee; for the month, he said, was gone.

"Nay, great Rishi," said Harischandra, "there remaineth half a day; await my payment thus far, I pray thee."

Then the king cast about wildly for some means to find the money; but there appeared to him no source of gain, save to sell his hapless wife and the boy into slavery. This she herself was the first to propose rather than allow her husband to lose his good name for truthfulness and incur the Brahman's curse. But so distraught was the king at her words, that he swooned away with grief; and when his senses returned, he could only cry shame on himself for bringing his wife to such a pass. The queen, beholding him swoon again, lamented over his woeful downfall, and, herself overwhelmed with pity for his misfortunes, fell fainting to the ground. The poor child, seeing his parents prone and helpless, and feeling the pinch of hunger, cried sadly on them for food.

Then came Viswamitra again, and, finding the king reft of sense, roused him with cold water, and urged him to pay with speed. Then at length the king, when Viswamitra was gone, cried, "Ho, citizens all! Behold me, a monster of ruthlessness, a very Rakshasa in human form, who am brought to selling my wife. If any desire her as a slave, let him speak quickly, while I have life to answer."

Then spake an aged Brahman, "My wife is very young and has need of help in the house. I am wealthy, and can pay ready money proportionate to thy wife's youth and beauty. Take the money, therefore, and deliver her to me." So saying, he paid over the money to the king, and, seizing the queen, dragged her away. The boy clung to his mother, and the Brahman at first drove him back with kicks; but the queen begged him to buy the boy also, as, parted from him, she would serve less diligently. So the Brahman added further money to his price, and bore the queen and her son away, leaving Harischandra to lament the vileness of a lot which forced him basely to sell those dearest to him as slaves.

Then came Viswamitra again and received the money; but, regarding it with scorn, he chid the king for the smallness of the gift, and vowed that

Harischandra would soon have proof of the might of Brahman sainthood, if he continued in the belief that such a sum was fit guerdon for a great sacrifice. Then, reminding the king that only a fourth part of the day remained, the sage took the money and departed.

Thereon Harischandra, all other means of gain gone from him, sorrowfully offered himself as a slave to any one that would buy him. At this there came forward a Chandala, or vile outcast, of loathsome appearance, ungainly gait and vulgar speech, bearing a skull in his hand and surrounded by a pack of dogs; withal, a hideous and repulsive figure. This man approached the king and bade him name his price. The king gazed on him in horror, and asked him his name.

"Pravira, I am called," answered the Chandala, "and in this city I am a slayer of the condemned and a gatherer of blankets from bodies of the dead."

Hearing this, Harischandra felt that death were better than the service of one so loathly; when, on a sudden, Viswamitra again appeared and demanded his fee in full. The king's piteous prayer for mercy was unregarded; the Rishi bade the hapless monarch sell himself to the Chandala for an hundred million pieces, or endure the blight of his curse. Then the king, bewildered, gave assent; and the Chandala, joyfully handing the money to Viswamitra, bound the king and led him, not without blows, to his foul abode.

There he bade the fallen Rajarshi go forth daily to the burning-grounds and collect the funeral clothes of the dead. "Day and night shalt thou watch for these; of what thou takest, such a part is for me, and such a part will be thy reward."

Who shall tell the horrors of a great Hindu burning-ground? None, at any rate, can describe the frightful scene more frightfully than do the Hindu legends themselves. For in these, beside the natural horrors of the place—the sights and smells, the heart-rending cries of relatives of the dead, the debased attendants, and dogs, jackals and vultures on their shocking quest—we read of foul and blood-thirsty fiends and imps of every kind thronging the scene of death and holding hellish orgies after their manner.

To this dolorous place came the fallen king, and, with woeful remembrance of the height whence he had fallen, applied himself to the sickening task of collecting the funeral wrappings of the dead, running hither and thither to one and another, reckoning carefully the proper division of his gruesome spoil. So heavy lay the spell of the place and the work upon him, that there and then the poor monarch entered into another birth, and became in deed what he seemed to be. Thus spending a dismal existence he fell one day, foredone with toil, into a deep sleep and dreamed a strange and dreadful dream. He saw himself passing from one sad existence to another; falling from even his present low estate to periods of anguish in various terrific places of torment. He saw himself once more born in his own order, a king again, only to lose his kingdom through dicing, bringing frantic misery on his wife and child. Then again there rang in his ears warnings about the dreaded curse of Viswamitra; and therewith the king awoke, inquiring, in his terror, whether all this time and dire experience had really passed over him. Then, ejaculating a prayer to the gods for deliverance, the king once more took up his wretched work.

Then there came to that burning-ground none other than his queen herself, with the body of the boy, who had perished by snake-bite. Neither of them recognised the other, for the king had become, as we have seen, wholly in appearance as one of the vile attendants of the burning-ground; while the queen was worn with the sorrow of long separation from her husband, and sadly marred by want and wandering. She, then, lamenting sorely, drew near to the funeral pyre; and Harischandra, noticing the kingly marks of the boy, thought sadly of the churlish fate by which one so like his own child had been thus early enthralled by dreadful death.

Then the queen, lamenting her fate in general, railed on the gods, saying, "Reft of kingdom and friends, wife and child sold into slavery, what has King Harischandra not suffered by the gods' decree?"

On hearing these words, the king recognised his wife, and crying aloud, "This is indeed my wife and child!" fell swooning to the earth. She, too, recognising her husband, all changed as he was, herself was overpowered with faintness. Anon they both recovered, and bewailed together the strange and hard lot that lay on them. The queen, scarce able to comprehend—even beholding with her eyes—her husband's miserable transformation and shameful toil, asked of him, saying, "Tell me, O king, do we wake or sleep? Art thou indeed as thou seemest?

If indeed it be so, then truth and righteousness are of no avail, and the worship of the gods profiteth not a whit."

Then the king, with sighs and faltering utterance, told his tale. The queen, too, related tearfully the story of the boy's death. Then these two together, dwelling on the hopelessness of their lot, determined to end their lives together; and the king, having laid his son on the heaped-up pyre, joined hands with his wife, and, meditating deeply on the Almighty, prepared to enter the blazing fire.

While he thus thought, Indra and all the gods, led by Dharma, drew near, and called to Harischandra, "Ho, lord king! behold us, gods and demigods, saints and sages, Nagas and Gandharvas! Here, too, is Viswamitra, whose enmity all three worlds have felt; but know that now he wishes thee well."

Thereon the king went up to meet this reverend company, and held converse with Indra, Dharma, and Viswamitra. "Noble Harischandra," said Indra, "ascend with wife and child to high heaven, hard indeed of access, but well earned by these thy virtues."

Then showers of nectar and heavenly flowers descended from on high, and celestial music sounded; the king's son, also, rose to life in fullness of health, and his father embraced him, while the queen, too, regained all her well-being. Then Indra bade them ascend forthwith; but King Harischandra, faithful even to the meanest duty, was fain to pause.

"King of gods," said he, "I may not go without rendering his due to my master, the head Chandala."

Then said Dharma, "Know that the Chandala was

myself, who, foreseeing thy affliction, took on me the disguise of a low outcast, to try thee."

Thereon Indra again called on them to ascend to heaven. But Harischandra, not forgetting, even in the joy of his escape from unmeasured sorrow, those towards whom his duty formerly lay, and who had loved him well, replied, "Suffer me, king of gods, with all humility to plead the cause of my loyal subjects, whom I may not lightly leave. For it is writ that to abandon one's dependants ranks with the most grievous sins. If they may come with me to Swarga, I go happily; if not, let me go rather to hell, so I be with them!"

"Bethink thee of their sins," said Indra, "for these are many."

"Even so," replied Harischandra, "'tis through the virtue of families, as much as by his own skill, that a king rules happily. Therefore, whatever merit is mine in respect of my ruling, be it reckoned as common to my citizens and me; and if it avail to carry me to heaven, let them be borne thither likewise."

"So be it," said Indra, Dharma, and Viswamitra. And therewith these heaven-dwellers sent word to the subjects of the king that they, too, should ascend with him; and this they did forthwith, moving in triumph from one heavenly chariot to another, amid the jubilations of the celestials. Great was the praise of Harischandra, who not only by his patience endured the sore trial laid on him by the sage's wrath, but also through loyal remembrance of his friends made them partakers of his own reward.

There was one, however, whom this happy ending

of the king's trials did not leave content. This was the great sage Vasishtha, who having been connected as priest with the house of Harischandra, was moved to exceeding hot anger when he heard how the virtuous king had been thrust from his kingdom and plagued by the overbearing pride of Gadhi's son.

"Even when Viswamitra slew my hundred sons," cried Vasishtha, "I was less wroth than I am this day, hearing how that pious, dutiful, and charitable monarch has been hurled from his throne and utterly brought low by that upstart. Now shall Viswamitra, blasted by my curse, be changed into a heron for his hardness of heart."

The sage's curse might not be gainsaid; but Viswamitra had not climbed, by centuries of toilsome penance, to the height of equality with the Brahmarshi, to bear his foeman's curse without full requital. He, therefore, retorted the curse with fury, and Vasishtha also was changed into a bird.

Then these two birds, of size monstrous beyond all belief, rose in the air and joined in bitter conflict. Before the wind caused by the blows of their huge wings, the mountains rocked and were overturned; the sea was lashed up from its very bottom, and overflowed into the nether regions; the world and all its inhabitants were exceedingly disquieted, and many creatures perished in the turmoil.

Then Brahma, father of gods and men, bade them take heed to the woe of the world and cease their strife, but at first they regarded not his words, and fought on. Again he drew near and, bidding them quit their assumed forms, he addressed them in their human shape, saying, "Stay, beloved Vasishtha, and thou, virtuous Viswamitra! By the strife which, in the darkness of your minds, ye wage, the world perishes; and this yielding to violent passion hath wrought grievous harm to the merits of both."

With that they stayed their strife, ashamed; and after embracing each other with love and forgiveness, they repaired each to his hermitage, and Brahma likewise departed to his place.

From these tales of Viswamitra and Harischandra, it may be seen what can be achieved by steadfast perseverance in the face of every obstacle; also, how, by patient endurance of adversity, a man may rise superior to the most cruel trials inflicted by a ruthless persecutor, and win in the end the favour of heaven and even the admiration and good-will of the oppressor.

Chapter II

THE TALE OF RAMA AND SITA

OF all cities in ancient Hindustan, few, if any, bore a prouder name than Ayodhya, the capital of the fair and fertile land of Kosala. Many miles it stretched in both length and breadth; its streets were broad and well laid out, its groves and gardens many and beautiful, its houses and palaces handsome and spacious. For all the multitude of its inhabitants, there was never dearth of any sort of food. Ayodhya's walls were strong, its army numerous and valiant, and many were its Brahman priests, famed for learning and liberality.

Over this goodly kingdom ruled Dasaratha, sprung from the royal Solar race. The justice of his rule was well seen in the prosperity of his subjects and in the general absence of sorrow and crime. The various castes devoted themselves faithfully to their proper duties, and all were obedient to the Brahmans, chief of whom was the great sage Vasishtha, the king's family priest. The king had three wives, Kausalya, Kaikeyi, and Sumitra; but his virtues seemed fated to die with him, for, alas! he had no son to succeed him.

To meet this constant source of sorrow, the king at length resolved to seek the favour of the gods by celebrating the famous Horse-sacrifice. The resolve pleased his counsellors well, and preparations were forthwith set on foot. A certain holy ascetic, whose ministry had proved of great value to another monarch on a like occasion, was invited to preside. Under the eye of Vasishtha, all things were duly got ready; kings and princes were invited, and assembled with much pomp and ceremony, and a full year after the making of the resolve—for such was the time appointed by sacred law—the sacrifice was begun with great solemnity, on the ground beyond the fair-flowing Sarayu, the river of Ayodhya. The chief queen, Kausalya, dealt the fatal blow, and then, as was the custom, passed the following night on the sacrificial ground. When all had been duly performed, Dasaratha distributed vast sums of money and other largesse to the attendant Brahmans; and these assured him that he would of a surety be blessed by the birth of four glorious sons.

Turn we from this to a matter very different, yet bearing closely on King Dasaratha's sacrifice and its consequences.

Far to the South, in the Isle of Lanka—now called Ceylon—dwelt the demon Ravana, king of the Rakshasas, or fiends. So great was the power of this grim being, that for fear of him the sun withheld his shining, the ocean forebore to stir, the winds did not dare to blow. The gods then came together to Brahma, the Creator, and begged him to devise means whereby the malice of this monster, running riot through the world, might be checked. To them Brahma answered that Ravana had won from him the boon that he should never be slain by god, demigod or demon; but, in his pride, Ravana had asked no safety from *man*. Thereon came Vishnu, the Preserver, and, when all had done him reverence, promised that he himself would become incarnate among men, and that by him in human form the fiend would be overthrown. Loud was the acclaim of the celestials, as the god thus promised, and with hymns of praise they sought to speed the fulfilment of his purpose.

Vishnu then descended to earth, and rose from Dasaratha's sacrificial fire in the guise of a strange monster, huge and black, all maned like a lion, bearing a golden vessel full of liquid. This he bade the king divide between his wives. To Kausalya, as chief queen, was given half; to the other two, a quarter each.

Then in due time were born the promised sons: to Kausalya, Rama, in whom was half the nature of Vishnu; to Kaikeyi, Bharat, who had a quarter of the divine nature; while to Sumitra came twins, Lakshman and Satrughna, who divided the remaining quarter between them. These children were born in an auspicious season, and grew up noble in body and well trained in every branch of the warrior's art and learned, also, in the study of the Vedas.*

The lads grew and throve apace, and in due time came the days when their sire must needs take thought for their marriage. At this season came the

* The earliest Hindu Scriptures. See Glossary.

famous sage Viswamitra, and sought the king's aid in a certain matter, and Dasaratha, ever prompt to succour holy men, gave consent without condition. The sage then expounded the matter, to wit, that he was sore hindered in the performance of religious rites by certain evil fiends. These he might slay by his own curse, at the time, but it were better that they should fall by a warrior's hand. To this end, Viswamitra begged of King Dasaratha the aid of his son Rama, to smite these foes, which, protected by the sage's care, the youth could safely do. Now Rama was but sixteen, and the king, sore troubled, was fain to refuse. Then Viswamitra was wroth, and threatened the king with ruin for breach of his plighted word. Vasishtha then urged Dasaratha to keep his promise, and Viswamitra further said that he possessed the secret of many mystical weapons, the mastery of which he would communicate to Rama. On this the king gave his consent; Rama, well prepared by Viswamitra, set forth in company with his brother Lakshman; the fiends were duly attacked and slain, and Rama emerged from his first warfare in triumph.

After this, Viswamitra suggested that they should go and see the wondrous bow of Janaka, King of Mithila. This bow, which the king had obtained from the god Siva for his sacrificial piety, neither demigod nor demon could bend, and the king had promised the hand of his lovely daughter Sita to him who should bend it. To Mithila, therefore, the princes and their adviser repaired; and there, on hearing of their coming, the king and his coun-

The Breaking of the Bow of Janaka 46

sellors came forth and received them with honour. From the Brahman Satananda the princes heard the story of Viswamitra's earlier days and his struggle with Vasishtha, the tale of which has been told.

Next day, Janaka bade men bring the bow for Rama and his brother to see. Many princes had striven to bend it, but all had failed. So huge it was that it had to be borne in a wagon drawn by stalwart men. But the youthful Rama, when it was shown to him, easily took the bow and strung it; then, while assembled thousands gazed in wonder—

> " *With steady aim the string he drew*
> *Till burst the mighty bow in two.*"

Dire was the clang of the bursting bow; the neighbourhood was shaken, and the spectators were stricken senseless.

Then Janaka, according to his promise, bestowed his daughter Sita upon Rama, and sent messengers to Ayodhya to invite Dasaratha. He, on receiving the glad news, set out in fitting state for Mithila, and was worthily received by Janaka, who had invited likewise his younger brother, Kusadhwaja, also a king. In view of the great importance of the marriage, the genealogy of either party was related in presence of the state assembly; Vasishtha recited that of Rama, while Janaka told his own. To complete the happiness of the occasion, Janaka bestowed his other daughter, Urmila, on Bharat, and to Lakshman and Satrughna were betrothed the two daughters of Kusadhwaja.

Then a dais with a fair canopy was raised, and

golden vessels, ladles, and censers were set in readiness, with barley, rice, water, and other things needful. The sacred fire was kindled in the midst, and Vasishtha performed the prescribed rites and gave the offering to the flame. Then Janaka led Sita forward and committed her to Rama, a faithful wife, to follow him as his shadow. The other princes and princesses were then in like manner joined in wedlock; thrice round the sacred fire went each bridal pair; and heavenly music and showers of blossoms crowned the ceremony.

Anon, Dasaratha and his sons with their brides returned to Ayodhya, where joyous crowds issued forth to meet them. After a time, Bharat and Satrughna were invited to visit for a season King Yudhajit, their uncle, while Rama and Lakshman remained at Ayodhya. Rama now began to share the government with his father, and daily increased in favour with all. As for the fair Sita, and the love they bore each other—

> "*He loved her for his father's voice*
> *Had given her and approved the choice;*
> *He loved her for each charm she wore,*
> *And her sweet virtues more and more.*
> *So he, her lord and second life,*
> *Dwelt in the bosom of his wife,*
> *In double form, that, e'en apart*
> *Each heart could commune free with heart.*
>
> . . . . .
>
> *Then shone the son Kausalya bore,*
> *With this bright dame allied,*
> *Like Vishnu whom the gods adore,*
> *With Lakshmi by his side.*"

II

Now King Dasaratha was very aged, and the burden of kingship weighed heavy on him. He was fain, therefore, to install his well-beloved Rama as heir and regent. This proposal brought joy to the hearts of all, nor did even Kaikeyi and Sumitra seek preference for their own sons, so dear to all had Rama made himself by his matchless skill in war, his gentleness and love of justice, his sympathy with the people, and other godlike virtues.

So the king's priests were bidden to make preparations for the joyful ceremony. The royal elephant, the tiger-skin, and white umbrella, were all in readiness, together with money for largesse, and stores of food for the people and guests, and all bade fair to turn out prosperously. But Dasaratha was ill at ease; his rest was troubled by frightful dreams, and the omens were evil. The great rite was appointed for a day which, it was thought, must surely be auspicious for Rama; and for this day the prince and Sita were bidden to prepare themselves by fasting and a night spent on a humble bed of sacred grass. The saint Vasishtha came to guide the fasting and meditation; after which Rama spent the night as directed, until but one watch of it remained. Then he arose and bathed, and, having had his house adorned, went forth, clad in a silken garment, to meet the duties of the memorable day. But memorable it was to be far otherwise than he or Ayodhya's citizens thought.

It chanced that among Kaikeyi's train was a humpbacked maid named Manthara, brought up with the queen herself. This girl, surveying from a staircase the joyful scene, asked of Rama's nurse, and was told, the cause of the festivities. Now this girl's mind was as ill-formed as her body; she hated Rama, and fury filled her heart when she learned that he was to be installed as heir and regent. She sought her royal mistress in haste, and roused her from sleep, crying, "Why sleepest thou, O Queen? Arise, for dire peril is upon thee!"

Rising dismayed, the queen asked what the dreaded ill might be. "Falsely," replied the maid, "hath he whom thou cherishest dealt with thee and thy son. The king, with serpent's guile, hath sent Bharat away, that in his absence Rama may be appointed heir-associate. Rouse thee, therefore, lest thou become in all things subject to Kausalya!"

But Kaikeyi's heart, thus far, was free of malice. No whit grieved by the news, she rather rejoiced thereat greatly, and gave the girl a jewel for her tidings, saying that Rama was dear to her as her own son Bharat.

Sore vexed, the girl cast the jewel from her in scorn, saying, "What folly is thine, O Queen, to dream of bliss, when, in truth, thou sinkest in seas of trouble! Truly, I tremble for thy son's welfare; he is the next heir to Rama, who will deem him all too near for safety. Thou, too, when Rama is enthroned, wilt be debased beneath Kausalya's feet."

Still the queen, vexed for Rama's sake, replied that he was the best of men, incapable of harming his brother, and as dutiful to herself as to his own mother. But the maid, with unabated malice, assailed her again with base charges against Rama, saying, "Be sure that, when Rama comes to power, Bharat will be driven from the land; and will Kausalya, whom of old thou didst despise and defy, forbear to try her rancour on a fallen rival?"

Too long Kaikeyi listened to the false tongue; the fire of jealousy was kindled in her heart, and her desire turned towards banishing Rama from the kingdom; but she must needs ask the girl how this might be compassed. Readily Manthara revealed her plan, saying—

"When, by thy care, King Dasaratha was healed of his wounds gotten in war with the demons, in gratitude he swore to grant thee a boon, not once, but twice. Now, therefore, recall his oath to the monarch's mind, and charge him forthwith to send Rama to the forest for twice seven years. In that space thy son will be stablished in the kingdom beyond fear of being moved. Hie thee now to the chamber of mourning, and, lying prostrate on the ground, refuse all comfort till the monarch grant thy prayer. Be bold and callous, and all is thine."

Swept away by the lust for pre-eminence, Kaikeyi hearkened to the evil persuasion of her maid, and praised the wisdom of the plan. Nay, made foolish by the foretaste of triumph, she praised even the appearance of the humpbacked maid, and promised her wealth of robes and jewels on the day when Bharat should become king in Rama's place.

Anon, stripping off every ornament, she cast herself on the cold floor of the dark mourning-chamber and awaited the fateful hour.

Meanwhile King Dasaratha, all things being in readiness, went forth to commune with his beloved

Kaikeyi on the joyful matter of the day now dawning. Through the lovely pleasure-grounds he passed, and came to her favourite apartment; but the couch whereon she loved to recline was empty, nor in all the bower could he spy aught of her graceful form. Then stood before him the damsel Manthara, and with folded hands told him, trembling, that the queen had sought the mourning-chamber in a passion of woe. Much moved, the king sought out the afflicted queen, and conjured her to declare the cause of her trouble. But Kaikeyi would tell nought till he had solemnly promised, as of old, to grant her boon; and he, distraught by the sight of her sorrow, swore by all the merit he had ever gained to grant what she asked, even were it the very heart in his breast.

Then the queen, her heart swelling with triumph to see him thus beguiled, replied, "Be all the gods my witnesses! Let sun, moon, and stars, the earth and all that therein is, take note of this oath and my demand! Remember, O King, how to me alone thou didst owe thy life, when stricken from the demon fray; and how thou swarest me a boon. I claim it now; and if thou refuse, I die this day. Let Rama depart forthwith, and for fourteen years dwell as a hermit in the woods; and let Bharat, my son, rule in his stead."

Scarce crediting the witness of his senses, the king stood amazed, as a deer in the presence of a tigress, marvelling whether some dream were upon him or some frenzy had smitten his mind. Then, as doubt departed, and the vile truth stood out inevitable, a cry of shame and horror broke from him, and he fell swooning to the ground. Scarce coming to himself, he plied her with every form of entreaty to take back the fell request, but all in vain. He flattered the queen on her beauty and good sense; he urged the rightfulness of Rama's claim, the completeness of the arrangements, the expectation of the citizens; he dwelt on his own forlorn state if deprived of Rama. But the queen only vowed that, if he did not meet her demand, she would that day drink poison before his eyes; and when Dasaratha, exhausted and desperate, fell again into a swoon, she, with no thought of pity, did but ask why he lay senseless, neglecting his plighted word. The king then arose, and wrathfully declared that Kaikeyi was no longer his true wife.

Meanwhile Vasishtha was sending word to Dasaratha to bid Rama come forth without delay, for the impending moment was most auspicious. Sumantra, the chief counsellor, was sent to fetch the prince, who thereon ascended a two-horse chariot, Lakshman standing behind him with the royal fly-whisk of yak's-tail. Rama found his father seated with Kaikeyi, and did obeisance to each in turn; but the hapless king could find no word but his son's name. Coldly the queen explained that Dasaratha was not angry, but was merely seeking to evade a promise made on oath to herself, which she would tell Rama when he had sworn to carry out the king's will in everything.

To this Rama replied that at his father's behest he would give up life itself. Then Kaikeyi told the prince that the king had promised to send him to the forests for fourteen years and to install Bharat as king. Rama dutifully accepted the mandate, and asked merely wherefore his father did not welcome him after the wonted fashion. But the stricken monarch, cut to the heart by the fulfilment of his odious duty, again sank insensible.

Wild was Kausalya's grief, and hot was Lakshman's ire, when Rama mildly imparted his heavy tidings to them. The mother cried that she had better have died childless, and that, if Rama departed, she would take her own life by fasting. Lakshman counselled resistance, and offered even to slay his father, if the cruel command was pressed.

Rama reasoned with each in turn. To Kausalya he said that, if bereft of her, the king would die, and that a woman's happiness stands and falls with her husband's welfare; therefore, she should neither take her own life nor come with her son to the forest. To her son's wise persuasion Kausalya yielded, and blessed his undertaking. But Lakshman still rebelled in spirit; Rama's obedience, whether to an unjust decree or to the overbearing might of fate, seemed to him childish and unworthy.

The dispossessed heir had next to carry word to his wife. Her he informed as gently as he could, and spoke of going alone to the forest, leaving her behind to pray for his welfare and comfort his mother. To this Sita replied, with much feeling, that she must needs go with him, for apart from him she had no support and cared not for life.

Rama again prayed her to stay, for the forest life was full of sorrow and danger. "The woods," said he, "are full of lions, elephants, and other wild monsters; the streams are deep and rife with crocodiles. Thy only bed will be a couch of leaves on the cold ground, in the midst of tangled thickets, full of snakes and scorpions. Be wise, therefore, love, and abide in the city!"

But Sita, with tears, replied—

> "*The perils of the wood and all*
> *The woes thou countest to appal,*
> *Led by thy love I deem not pain;*
> *Each woe a charm, each loss a gain.*"

"With thee beside me, such trials will be no trials. I married thee to be thy wife and helper, and faithful attendance on thee is my surest path to bliss, both here and hereafter. But know, if thou refuse my plea, I shall by drowning, fire, or poison, end the life I may not spend by my husband's side."

To these and other entreaties Rama at length gave ear, and promised that she should go with him. She was bidden to distribute her wealth to Brahmans and servants; so the twain made ready to depart. Then Lakshman, when his talk of resistance found no favour, said he would in any case go with them; and Rama, at first unwilling to take his brother from home, at length consented, and gave Lakshman command concerning the weapons that should be taken.

It would take long to tell with any fullness of the arrangements that had to be made; of the many messages that passed between the royal parents and their children, between the departing ones and Vasishtha, Sumantra, and others; of the universal lamentation in the city, and the expressions of sorrow that rose from all save Kaikeyi, whose unblushing joy and triumph drew on her the sternest rebuke of the august Vasishtha.

The hour of departure came, and Rama and his small following left Ayodhya's walls. On the first day's journey crowds followed them, even to the banks of a river where they encamped for the night; but Rama and his party rose early in the morning, while others slept; and, crossing the river, they so guided their course that the people lost track of them, and returned, bewildered and weeping, to their homes. Then Rama and the others, faring swiftly on through the land of Kosala, crossed the river Gomati, and, casting a last glance towards Ayodhya, bade the city a long farewell.

When they came to the swift-flowing Ganges they were met by Guha, king of the Nishadas, who sent for boats to convey them across. They then went on to the place where the Yamuna—now called Jumna—joins the Ganges; here stands now the town of Allahabad, much esteemed by Hindus as a place of pilgrimage. Near the confluence of these rivers lived a holy sage; him Rama and his companions visited, and he counselled them to seek Chitrakuta—"Peak of many colours"—as an hermitage. Thither, accordingly, on the next day they bent their course. Rama bade Lakshman prepare a cottage thatched with leaves, and offerings were made to gain the good-will of the various gods. So fair was the spot that in its varied charms the exiles well-nigh forgot the sorrows of their fate.

Sumantra, the chief counsellor, who had accompanied them for some distance, left them ere they reached their goal, and regained Ayodhya on the third day after leaving them. All was sad and drear in the city, deserted by him who had been the light of every eye. More cavillings arose in the royal household concerning the king's consent to Kaikeyi's baneful demand; but Dasaratha, while owning his folly in so wildly promising whatever Kaikeyi might ask, now pointed out that the evil was, in truth, a punishment brought on him by a former sin. Once, in his youth, he had gone forth with bow and arrows to hunt and, mistaking the sound of a pitcher filling for the movements of an elephant, he had shot in that direction and wounded to death the water-carrier, a young man, the son of an aged couple. When Dasaratha bore the news to them, the father laid on him the curse that he should die from grief for his son, and therewith the parents departed this life. So now, said Dasaratha, the curse had come upon him; his senses began to fail; and, cursing Kaikeyi as his family's foe, he breathed his last.

When the first grief of the widowed queen was past, Vasishtha declared that Bharat must at once be summoned. Trusty envoys were sent off, and, travelling apace, they came in good time to the capital of King Yudhajit, where Bharat and Satrughna were sojourning.

On that night, Bharat himself was vexed with fearful dreams. He seemed to see his sire, pale and dishevelled, plunge from a mountain-top into a horrible pool of filth; again, the king appeared in strange guise, borne southward in a car drawn by asses, and mocked by a grisly fiend. Bharat foreboded nought but ill from these visions, deeming that his father or one of his brothers must surely perish ere long.

Even while he spake of these things in the palace,

the envoys from Ayodhya arrived. The message summoning Bharat was given, the travelling gear was got together, farewells were said and parting gifts bestowed, and Bharat set forth with speed. After seven days' journeying, they spied Ayodhya afar. From that great city rose usually a mighty hum, heard far off; but now no such sound greeted the ears of the approaching prince. His nearer sight and entry of the city served but to increase his fears. The streets and houses were ill-kept, and such folk as were seen abroad walked sadly with downcast eyes. Full of dismay, Bharat made his way to Kaikeyi's palace, and, after receiving her embrace, asked news of his sire, only to learn that the king was sped. Kaikeyi strove to stay the young man's grief; but when he learned, in reply to further questions, that Rama had gone to the forests and that his mother had been the cause thereof, he rose and denounced her as the murderess of the king, a fiend in human shape, worthy only to be driven to the forests, or to perish by fire or rope.

Hearing that Kaikeyi's son was come, Kausalya sent word to bring him to her. Bitterly at first she greeted him, taunting him with having gained Rama's kingdom by his mother's guile. But Bharat, falling at her feet, solemnly cursed all who had had part in causing Rama's banishment; whereon the queen was comforted and welcomed Bharat with affection.

The funeral of Dasaratha having been performed with fitting pomp, Bharat and Satrughna were mournfully speaking together of their great loss, when the maid Manthara, now bedizened with every sort ot gaud and ornament, passed by and gazed upon them. Straightway the brethren laid hands on her, and Satrughna so beat her that his brother exclaimed: "A woman may not be slain, or myself should have done the deed. Were Rama to hear that the humpbacked wench had been slain, it would please him ill." So they suffered her to depart.

Anon came the folk to beg Bharat to take the reins of government in his hands, but he refused, and commanded, instead, that an army should be got ready to go forth to Rama's forest dwelling, to escort him home as king, while he himself would remain in the woods. This pious resolve was greeted with reverent admiration, and all bent them to the work of preparing. When all was ready, a great multitude set out in company with the army. At the River Ganges, King Guha, seeing the great host, at first thought that Bharat had gathered this puissance to follow Rama and slay him; wrath filled his heart, and he took thought to bar the passage of the river by force. But when he learned the high purpose of Bharat's coming, he cried with delight to the prince, "Blessed art thou! None on earth know I to rival thee, O prince!"

On the next morning, therefore, Guha had five hundred boats made ready to give passage to Bharat's host, who, after taking leave of the king, proceeded to the hermitage where Rama's party also had halted. The sage greeted Vasishtha with honour; to Bharat, after divers questions on either hand, he said, "Why art thou here? I misdoubt me somewhat of thy coming, lest, haply, knowing that thy brother has been banished for twice seven years, thou be come after him with all thy following to do him harm."

"That be far from me!" cried Bharat sorrowfully. "Lost indeed were I, could I harbour such foul intent in my breast. The guilty demand of my mother, foolishly jealous on my behalf, found no approval from me. I seek my brother's abode only to throw myself at his feet and lead him back to reign; tell us, therefore, where he abides."

So the saint, well pleased, told Bharat of Rama's dwelling on Chitrakuta. He then bade the prince bring up his army, that he might give them goodly entertainment. Every kind of attractive food and drink was produced by the saint's power and prayers, and all feasted to their heart's content, celestial choristers made music, and heavenly nymphs danced before Bharat and his host. So ravished were the greater part by this royal cheer that they spoke of staying in such a heavenly place, neither advancing to the forest nor returning to Ayodhya.

Next morning, however, came the word to advance; all, therefore, saluted the noble hermit, the three queens likewise coming forward to do farewell obeisance. Bharat reddened with anger when talk of his mother arose; but the sage bade him control his wrath, as the banishment of Rama would yet end in the benefit of all.

Approaching Chitrakuta, they discerned, after some survey, the region of Rama's dwelling, by rising smoke. Bharat thereon left the body of the host and went forward, with Sumantra only, to meet his brothers.

During these early days of his banishment Rama took great delight in exploring, with his beloved Sita, the beauties of Chitrakuta—the peak bright with many colours. The woods abounded with flowers and fruit of every sort, and the beasts of the forest roamed free from all fierceness. Fair streams plashed down the mountain's sides, and birds made music everywhere. In the midst of these charms the hearts of Rama and his wife were consoled, and they ceased to pine for Ayodhya and royal estate.

On a day, however, when Rama led Sita by the goodly stream Mandakini, dotted with islets, frequented by ducks and cranes, with herds of deer drinking fearlessly at its margin, Bharat's host approached with much sound and dust, scaring the forest denizens far and wide. Spying from a tree, Lakshman made out the great company of men, horses, and elephants, and in the midst of all he discerned the cognisance of Bharat. Therewith came to him the thought that had at first assailed both Guha and the hermit, to wit, that Bharat had gathered this army to put out, once for all, his brother's claim to the throne; and bitter wrath flooded Lakshman's soul. Fiercely he cried that they should resist amain; that, if they thus stood, Bharat might well fall before their stroke, and Kaikeyi, the plotter of the mischief, perish also, while the slopes of Chitrakuta ran with the blood of sinners.

But Rama, ever wise as bold and righteous as brave, replied, "What should I gain, brother, when I have sworn to carry out this my father's command? Methinks, indeed, Bharat hath but come to visit us in friendship. He hath never done thee wrong, and would, I doubt not, make over the kingdom to thee thyself at my behest, shouldst thou desire it."

With these words Lakshman's foolish wrath was shamed; then he said, "Surely it is our father who comes to visit us!" But Rama doubted somewhat, seeing, indeed, the royal elephant but not the royal sunshade.

Bharat, meanwhile, searched not in vain for his brother's haunt. And, having made sure of his way, he bade Vasishtha call the queens. Then he himself sped on to Rama's forest dwelling, the cottage of leaves, floored with grass, wherein sat Rama in raiment of barkcloth, with Sita and Lakshman by his side. Much moved was Bharat by the sight of these princely ones thus humbly housed and attired; while Rama, in turn, scarce recognised his brother, so worn was Bharat with sorrow and anxious care. Many questions passed between them; Rama inquired much concerning the welfare of all in Ayodhya, while Bharat besought his brother, with every kind of entreaty, to return to the capital and be installed as king. Nought had Bharat said thus far of the old king's death; now, sadly, he broke the grievous news, as a last argument to enforce his petition that Rama should return and take the kingdom to himself. The word of his father's death came on Rama as the blow of the axe that fells the tree. Down he fell unconscious, and when he came to himself he cried that he would not return to Ayodhya even when his time of exile was over. Then the brothers and Sita made a funeral offering to the spirit of the departed king, and made great lamentation together; the noise of their weeping was heard by the host, and sorrow came upon them all.

Then drew near the sage Vasishtha with the queens, who looked sadly on the lowly surroundings of Rama and his party, and lamented the cruel lot that bound the prince to exile and Lakshman to the work of a servant.

Next morning the brothers met quietly in the presence of the army, and all were curious to hear how Bharat would address his brother. Then Kaikeyi's son said calmly, "The kingdom was bestowed on me at my mother's request. It is mine to give—I yield it to thee. Take it, then, for thou alone art worthy to hold it!"

But Rama answered, "Be wise, brother, and cease to strive with Fate, which is stronger than all. My word to my father may not be recalled. As for him, too, let us not bewail his lot overmuch. He is gone, as all perforce must go; but he is gone full of days and honour to the abode of the righteous in heaven, and this we should not mourn. Turn thee, therefore, and reign in Ayodhya; I, for my part, abide here, obedient to our sire's command."

Filled with admiration for his brother's calm faithfullness, Bharat replied, "O conqueror of foes, where is thy peer, whom pain doth not daunt nor joy uplift? Yet shouldest thou ascend the throne; for our father was in dotage when he yielded to my mother; and thy duty as a Kshatriya bids thee wear the crown. But if thou refuse, I shall remain with thee in the forest."

All present praised Bharat's words and joined their prayers with his. But Rama, while doing honour to his brother's nobility of purpose, still kept his heart unmoved. Then came a Brahman, Javali by name, and, with the plea that the dead are gone and done with and cannot bind our actions, sought to tempt the steadfast prince. But Rama rebuked his words, as savouring of impiety; whereon Javali said that he had used the plea only to test Rama's faithfulness, and that he himself scorned such ungodliness.

In the end Bharat consented to return to Ayodhya, on the condition that he might take with him Rama's sandals to set up in token that he only held the government from Rama's hand. Having received the sandals, he then bade Rama a mournful farewell; then, bearing the sandals on his head in token of allegiance, he ascended his car and the return journey was begun. Reaching Ayodhya in due course, he set up the sandals as determined, and then withdrew to dwell in a village somewhat to the east of the city.

Soon after Bharat left, Rama and Sita learned from some of the hermits who lived around that the neighbourhood was infested with loathsome fiends, who delighted to put every hindrance in the way of those engaged in pious acts. At the request of these ascetics, Rama and his wife removed their abode, and accompanied them to the Dandaka forest. Even here, however, they were not to remain unmolested. A terrific Rakshasa, named Viradha, carried off Sita in the presence of Rama and Lakshman, telling them that a boon from Brahma made him safe against death from any weapon. The brethren then fought against him for some time with small avail; but when Viradha seized them up and bore them away, they broke his arms and brought him to the ground. Then they made an end of him by burying him alive.

Moving from one hermitage to another, they passed ten years happily enough. They foregathered with many holy sages, and spent a few months at each place in turn, enjoying the beauties of these calm retreats, amid flowery woods frequented by harmless beasts and birds of melodious song. In particular, they had great joy in their communing with the Rishi Agastya, from whom they got great store of good counsel and encouragement. The saint bade them not doubt that all their trials would end in a change of fortune, and commended for an abode a pleasant woodland named Panchavati, not many miles from his own hermitage. To this place they went, and chose for their dwelling a lovely spot near the goodly river Godavari; here they built a simple but comfortable cottage, and settled down to live in great happiness. But the beginning of great troubles was near at hand.

III

One day, when Rama was sitting with Sita and Lakshman, Surpanakha, sister of the Rakshasa king Ravana, passed by, and was smitten with love for the handsome prince. Though vile and hideous herself, she hesitated not to go forward and entreat Rama to leave Sita and marry herself. At first Rama answered with jests, and bade her woo his brother. Lakshman, in turn, treated the matter jestingly; but when the Rakshasi, in a fury, attacked Sita, he drew his sword and cut off her nose and ears. In this woeful plight, Surpanakha fled shrieking, and sought the aid of her brother Khara. He, on hearing her tale, first sent fourteen huge Rakshasas to avenge his sister's wrongs; but Rama slew them all. Surpanakha, who had witnessed the conflict, brought word to Khara, and urged him with prayers and taunts to go forth and slay their foe.

On this Khara summoned Dushana, another brother, and bade him gather a great host of Rakshasas, bent on evil. Terrible omens occurred as Khara and his army went forth; but, mad with wrath, the giant heeded not, and pressed on, swearing that his sister would drink the blood of Rama and Lakshman that very day.

Gods, saints, and other celestial beings drew near to see the fight and to wish Rama good fortune. Then the Rakshasa host, headed by Khara, advanced to battle with great uproar. Hemmed in on every side, Rama nevertheless overcame his foes by means of his mystic weapons, which caused the air to be darkened with clouds of darts and arrows, and destroyed the fiends by hundreds and thousands. Dushana advanced furiously to the fray and engaged Rama in single combat; but he was helpless before the hero's might, and was quickly slain. Finally Khara himself, though daunted by his brother's fall, rushed to the attack and pierced Rama with many arrows. Rama, in return, pierced Khara's steeds and charioteer, and wounded his foe. Then Khara seized a mace and hurled it like a thunderbolt at Rama; but Rama checked it in mid-air, so that it fell harmless to the ground. After further furious conflict, Rama began gradually to prevail.

"Then from his side a shaft he took
Whose mortal stroke no life might brook:
Of peerless might, it bore the name
Of Brahma's staff, and glowed with flame:
Lord Indra, ruler of the skies,
Himself had given the glorious prize."

Before this dire weapon the demon warrior fell slain; the heavenly minstrels beat their drums, and all the celestial visitants did homage to the victor.

From the overthrow of the Rakshasa host there escaped but one, by name Akampana, to bear tidings to Ravana, their king. Him Akampana advised not to challenge the puissant Rama in battle, but to carry off Sita.

"Reft of his darling wife, be sure,
Brief days the mourner will endure."

Pleased with his plan and enflamed by the taunts of Surpanakha, the Rakshasa lord determined to set forth. Terrible indeed was the might of Ravana. He had ten faces and twenty arms, and his body was seamed with scars received in battle with gods who had failed to overthrow him. He had ravaged the realm of the Nagas in the underworld, and stolen thence the bride of the Serpent-king himself; from Kailasa he had borne away the car of Kuvera, the god of wealth; he had despoiled the paradise of Indra, and the groves of the Gandharva king. Neither god nor demigod, Naga nor Gandharva, could work him ill. *Man* alone had he forgotten to name in the boon he had won from Brahma, that none should be able to do him to death, and what man was he that should stand against such as

Ravana? For all his might, however, Ravana first sought the dwelling of the Rakshasa Maricha, who dwelt as a hermit beneath a mighty fig-tree in a holy wood. To him Ravana set forth his purpose, and asked him to aid in carrying off Rama's lovely wife. "Let Maricha," said he, "take the form of a golden deer with silver spots, and wander where Sita might see him; then would she bid Rama and Lakshman catch the wondrous deer, and in their absence he, Ravana, would bear the helpless Sita away."

Pale grew Maricha as the demon king unfolded his plan. He knew, better than Ravana, the matchless power of Rama, and he urged his lord not to draw the tempest of ruin on his head by seeking to carry off Sita.

"Once," said the Rakshasa hermit, "I roamed the earth, strong as a thousand Nagas, slaughtering ascetics and feeding on their flesh, in the Dandaka forest. Then went the holy Viswamitra, and begged of King Dasaratha the aid of young Rama against me and my comrades; and the monarch, though loth to send his beloved son, then but twelve years old, was overborne by the Rishi's entreaty. Proud of my strength, I bore down upon Rama with a murderous axe; but he, a beardless boy, abode my onset unmoved, and with a single invincible shaft hurled me, stricken and senseless, far into the ocean. Saved from thence, I made my way to Lanka; but my comrades perished one and all. Take heed, therefore, from my fate, and beware of seeking to lay hands on Sita. Wives thou hast, many and fair—be content with them. If thou seekest to tear the fair daughter of Janaka from Rama's side, thine eyes will see Lanka in ruins, and thou and thine will fall before the hero's unerring shafts. Of his prowess I have other proof beside what I have told; be patient, therefore, and provoke him not. If I must do thy bidding, I shall not flinch, though certain death will be my fate. One word more—say, my lord, what wrong hath Rama done to thee thyself? Pause, then, ere thou bring his wrath upon thee; lest, when he bends his bow at length, thou and all thy chosen warriors fall slain before him."

But Ravana, scorning Maricha's wise advice, answered with disdain, "Is this counsel worthy of the giant race? This Rama is a weakling fool, who, at a woman's call, left his kingly duty to dwell in the woods. His wife will I easily bear away, and neither god nor demon shall stay me. A wise counsellor frames his speech with prudence, and, if he would say aught that may displease his lord, conveys it by a cautious hint. But thy words to thy royal liege are blunt and bitter, and could win no assent, even were they true. I did but ask thy help: this give, and prate not of Rama's strength and mine. Change thy form to that of the golden deer, and lure Rama from his beloved's side; and, if he bid Lakshman stay to guard her, then, when thou hast drawn Rama far from the hermitage, assume his voice and cry aloud, 'Ho, Lakshman! Ho, my Sita!' Hearing the cry, Lakshman will fly to the rescue, and Sita, deserted, will be my prey."

Thus overborne, Maricha yet replied boldly, "Who, my lord, is the vile wretch that has thus urged thee to that which will surely be thy bane? Wise counsellors ever do their best to restrain a monarch bent on folly; but thine, alas, see the danger, yet seek not to save thee from ruin. Even when the righteous perish, it must often be that many fall with them; how dreadful, then, the ruin which is brought about by the headstrong folly of the cruel and wicked! For myself I care not—my death will doubtless be the first—but I grieve for the giant race and for Lanka. Farewell to all our life and glory, if thou dare to lay hand on Rama's wife!"

Then, seeing his words fell idly on Ravana's ear, he bestirred himself, resigned to fate, to go with his lord and do his bidding. Aloft the magic car bore the twain, and brought them, over plain and hill, over city and river, to the spot where Rama's cottage stood. Then swiftly Maricha doffed his proper form and took on the guise of the wondrous deer. His golden coat, flecked with silver, was gay with many jewel tints, and sapphires tipped his branching horns. Now browsing on the tender foliage, now gambolling gaily with graceful leaps and bounds, he passed into the sight of Sita, as she returned from the woods to the cottage, culling the blooms from many a flowering shrub and tree. Amazed she saw the magic deer, and called to Rama and Lakshman to come and admire it. Swiftly came the brethren and gazed eagerly upon it; but Lakshman's heart was full of doubt, and he said, "I fear this is none other than the fiend Maricha, who has often donned this guise to beguile and slay kings while hunting. No deer on earth was ever seen thus gay with jewel tints; this is nothing less than sorcery."

But Sita, loth to forego the chance of such rare spoil, still besought her husband to catch the fairy

Fr. "Amazed she saw the Magic Deer"

beast and take it alive, to charm them during the days of their forest retreat and then to grace the palace grounds at Ayodhya after their return; or, if it could not be taken alive, to strike it down and bring its skin. Thus pressed, and himself beguiled by the loveliness of the strange beast, Rama turned to his brother and said, "Truly, brother, this deer were a kingly prize and well worthy of my hand. And again, if it be in truth, as thou dost surmise, the fiend Maricha, I am the more set on the death of one who has wrought such wickedness. To the chase, then, I hasten; do thou abide here and guard my Sita jealously, providing for every chance and alert for foes on every side."

So saying, he seized bow and arrows, and strode forth in pursuit of the deer, which fled trembling. From brake to brake it lured him, now seen close at hand, now lost to view, ever leading him farther from his home. Wroth at this constant failure to take the beast alive, Rama laid to his bow a magic shaft and sent it hissing to the heart of the deer. Loud roared the dying giant, dropping in the hour of death his borrowed form; then, mindful of his lord's behest, he gathered his ebbing strength and cried amain in Rama's voice, "Ho, Lakshman! Ho, my Sita!" and so gave up the ghost.

Then Rama perceived that this was in very deed a fiendish wile, back flew his mind in anxious thought for Sita; a creeping horror pressed on his heart, and, hastily slaying a buck for food, he hastened back to the hermitage.

But the cry of the dying Rakshasa had done its work too well. Hearing the agonised call in the well-known tones, Sita wildly called on Lakshman to run to her husband's aid; and when Lakshman refused to leave her, she goaded him cruelly with passionate taunts, saying that he had been seized with base desire to have her for his own wife and would gladly stand by, unmoved, while Rama perished. Against this storm Lakshman bore himself bravely and humbly; he bade her have confidence in Rama's might, which no living thing could quell, and said that he himself would suffer every reproach rather than break his word. But to the continued fury of Sita's tongue he yielded at length; sadly he gazed on her, and then, with dire foreboding, went forth to seek Rama.

IV

Then drew near the ten-faced lord of Lanka with fell intent. The winds forbore to blow as he came, and every leaf in the forest was still with fear. But he first appeared in the humble guise of a Brahman mendicant, whom the princess might receive as a revered guest. Deeply smitten by her beauty, as she sat weeping for the absent ones, he addressed her thus with courteous speech, "Who art thou, fair one, thus strangely lost in forest gloom? Art thou the Queen of Love, descended from on high, or some spirit of Fame or Beauty? Ne'er have I seen thy peer on earth. What shame that thou shouldst waste thy fairness on this wild retreat! A palace were fitter setting for such a jewel. How comes it that one so fair dwells unguarded in the dread forest?"

In reply, Sita, deceived by the false mendicant's appearance, and fearful lest he should curse her if she did not answer, related her story in full, asking him, in turn, his name and race and why he wandered thus in the forest.

Then said he, "O Sita, I am Ravana, lord of the Rakshasa hosts! Be thou my love, fair one, in my island city of Lanka, where five thousand maids shall wait on thee, and no sadness or pain shall ever come near thee!"

Then Sita's wrath broke forth on him. "Fool!" she cried, "to dream that such as thou shouldst chance to win Rama's wife. Better for thee to tear the prey from the famished lion, to pluck the fangs from an angry snake, to drink poison; sooner wilt thou swim the sea with a millstone around thy neck, or pluck the sun and moon from heaven, or cherish burning fire in thy garment, than steal the loyalty of Rama's spouse. *Thou* seek to fill Rama's place? As the lion to the jackal, as the eagle to the crow, as heavenly nectar to the dregs of rice-water, so is Rama, my husband, compared with thee!"

Thus scornfully she flung her answer to the Rakshasa king; but all the while she trembled like a reed, and Ravana, watching closely, marked the same with fierce exultation. Then, to quell her spirit yet more, he recounted all his titles to greatness, his mastery of gods and demons, his dominion over wind and wave, and all the resources of his kingdom. He bade her beware lest, if she refused his loving offer, the sad fate of the nymph Urvasi should overtake her; and he boasted that his little finger was more than a match for all Rama's might in battle.

It were a pity to pass by the name of Urvasi, of whom Ravana spake to Sita, without some word of her strange history. So, as the tale is no long one, it may well be told shortly here.

The Tale of Pururavas and Urvasi

The story is one related in many of the Hindu scriptures, and hence it comes that it is given with many differences in the various tellings. In any case, the greater share of sorrow seems to have fallen rather on Pururavas than on Urvasi, though Ravana meant Sita to think chiefly of her sufferings.

This Urvasi was one of the nymphs of heaven, the choice companion of the Gandharvas and other celestial beings, while Pururavas was a king of ancient days of wide-spread fame and dominion.

To follow one tale, this fair nymph fell under the curse of certain gods, and was condemned to undergo a period of abasement to earth, not without suffering while she was there. Then it chanced that an audacious Daitya, named Kesin, drew near to Indra's palace, and from the very portal bore the hapless nymph away. To avenge this insult and recover Urvasi, Indra invoked the service of the noble King Pururavas, who forthwith went out to battle with the Daitya hosts. Them he overthrew by his great might, and returned triumphant, bearing in his car the victim of the demon's raid, trembling but unharmed. Small wonder was it, then, that thereafter the fairest of the heavenly beauties and her royal rescuer became smitten with mutual love;

ere long the matter became public, and the twain were wedded in great happiness.

Then unhappily, it chanced that as, in the early rapture of their espousal, through certain fair woodlands, the nymph yielded to some small motion of jealousy, and turned from her husband's side to go her wilful way for a space. In this reckless wandering she strayed, unchecked now by her lord's wise counsel, into some lands sacred to the war-god and forbidden to the foot of woman. For this trespass she was changed into a wild vine, clinging round a tree stem, until the appointed time of her punishment should pass.

A woeful time it was for both, and wildly did King Pururavas search far and near, high and low, for the bride so soon parted from him. Many a long day he plied his frantic quest; till in a cleft of rock he spied a gem of wondrous brilliance, a ruby rich and rare. Yet, in his sorrow, he took small count of even this glorious jewel, and would have passed it by, when a heavenly voice bade him take the gem, which should prove to him the key of his difficulty. So he passed on his way with lightened cheer, and came anon to a vine that caught his eye. Wasted by some sad blight, it seemed to picture his own pitiful condition, and, giving voice to his thought, he stretched out his arms yearningly towards the drooping creeper; when lo, in presence of the magic ruby the spell was broken, and his Urvasi once more stood before him in the flesh. Of their happy re-union small need to speak at length.

From the point where it was said that Urvasi was condemned to be abased for a season from heaven, the tale is also told thus. King Pururavas having won the nymph's affection, it became a matter of no small concern to the Gandharvas and other celestial beings that their dearest companion should be parted from them so long. They therefore imposed certain conditions on the union of the mortal and the heavenly nymph.

Urvasi took with her to earth two rams of heavenly breed, which she cherished even as a mother her children; these, it was agreed, Pururavas should ne'er suffer to be parted from her. Also it was laid down that the monarch should never be seen unrobed by his bride. And the shrewd celestials perceived that through these conditions they might, almost when they would, compel their Urvasi to leave the world of mortals.

Thus, when the Gandharvas wearied of long separation from their dear playmate, certain of them went by night and stole the rams—first one, then the other—from Urvasi's chamber. At the cries of the first the king awoke, but feared to rise unrobed; but when to the cries of the second Urvasi added her own, conjuring her husband to fulfil his promise to prevent the rams being parted from her, he sprang from his couch and seized his sword to assail the robbers. Then the Gandharvas caused a flash of lightning to make the darkness as daylight, and Urvasi, beholding her spouse scantily attired, passed at once from his sight and returned to her own world.

Pururavas, thus bereaved, passed his time in woe and lamentation. But after a season he came on his beloved, sporting by a fountain with some of her comrades. Then she agreed to descend to earth for one night in each year; and to them were born, in time, six sons—though some say eight. But Pururavas wearied of this strange wedlock, and he yearned that they might be together always. And at length the Gandharvas, pitying the greatness of his yearning, offered him whatever boon he should choose; and it is not hard to guess his choice. Thereon they bade him perform certain rites, with his mind fixed on Urvasi; and this rite, somewhat changed, having been performed, Pururavas won for himself a place in the world of the Gandharvas, and was never again parted from his love.

There are those who say that this most ancient story is but a parable of nature. Some see in Pururavas and Urvasi the sun and the dawn; others hold that Pururavas is the sun, and Urvasi the morning mist, which vanishes even as the sun gains heat, attracted and yet dissipated by his beams.

However this may be, the tale is a most ancient one, and is sung in the old Veda itself in a form which shows that it was already a story well-known and understood. As for the fitness of the tale to Ravana's purpose, perchance it was even nearer the mark than the giant intended; for Pururavas and Urvasi, though woefully parted for a season, won through their sorrows and were happily re-united in the end.

When Sita spurned him as before, Ravana rose terrific before her in his own demoniac form, and, after one vain cry for mercy from her, seized her round the waist and bore her aloft in air. Loud and shrill her cry for help arose, but all too far off to reach Rama and Lakshman. One helper, however, was at hand; on a tree hard by reposed the giant vulture Jatayus, himself of Rakshasa blood, but kindly disposed, and friendly to Rama and Sita. On him did Sita call, and at her cry he woke. First he sought to turn Ravana from his cruel and base attempt by persuasion—for he and Ravana were of common stock—but when the Ten-faced mocked him and his counsel, he swung aloft in air and prepared to do battle for the right. With rending talons and savage blows of his wings he tare and smote the demon king; but Ravana, though cumbered in the fight by having to hold Sita fast, was yet too mighty for his staunch assailant, and triumphing in the end, bore away his prize secure, leaving the vulture gasping in the throes of death.

Thick darkness overspread the sky at the lawless deed. Brahma, the Creator, exclaimed on high, "The deed is done!" Gods and saints bewailed Sita's suffering; yet joy strove with their sorrow, for they knew that now had begun that course of events which would surely lead to Ravana's downfall. Fair and sad she was borne through the air in the grasp of the fiend, her beauty showing on his huge and hideous bulk like the pale moon rising through a murky autumn cloud, and the flowers dropping from her neck fell on his dark brows like stars encircling the crown of Mount Meru. The birds of the air flocked together, and the trees bowed their heads to wish her comfort. But Ravana's flight was not stayed. The sun himself, the glorious lord of day, was dismayed that wrong should thus seem to triumph over right, and from all nature there rose a sound of loud lament.

Once more did Sita change her tone from prayer to warning, foretelling the spoiler's overthrow and doom. But neither prayer nor warning might check him now, and onward through mid-air he sped cherishing the prize doomed to be his bane,

> "*Like the rash fool who hugs beneath*
> *His robe a snake with venomed teeth.*"

At length the giant came to the land's end, and passing high o'er the foaming waves of the sounding strait, he hovered over Lanka's isle and city. Descending into the midst thereof, he gave Sita into the charge of Rakshasi attendants; but he commanded that nothing which she asked for should be denied, and swore that any who troubled her should die the death. Then he appointed eight grim Rakshasas, of approved prowess, to go forth and gain tidings of Rama's doings.

Anon Ravana repaired to Sita again, and sought to win her by new blandishments. He showed her the brightest chambers, gleaming with gems and work of gold, the fairest pleasure-grounds, and all the goodness of his house; but she, sunk in grief, heeded not. He vaunted the greatness of his might and the number of his subjects, and begged her to become queen over all, admonishing her to put away all hope of seeing Rama again. He pleaded with her to believe that such a union could bring no shame; and, kneeling before her, placed her feet upon his head, in token of his heart's utter subjection to her charms.

But Sita, with new-kindling wrath, spurned him

more disdainfully than ever, and fearlessly extolled her husband's worth and might. Ravana, cried she, had sealed his country's doom, and widowed Lanka would soon run with Rakshasa blood. Thus repulsed, Ravana glowed with fury, and fiercely told her that if she would not change her word, his cooks should mince her flesh for his morning meal. Therewith he bade the Rakshasis take her in hand and tame her pride; and these foul dames led her forth to the palace gardens, and watched her as tigers watch a deer, with many a horrid taunt and threat.

V

Maricha being slain, Rama hastened back towards the hermitage in great anxiety of mind. Evil omens disturbed him as he went, and as he drew nearer home he noted with dismay that birds and beasts seemed filled with confusion and terror. Anon came Lakshman hurrying to meet him; but it was no welcome that Rama gave him, saying, "Why hast thou left the princess? I fear that all imports some fiendish scheme to lure both thee and me from Sita's side."

Lakshman heard his brother's reproaches with downcast eye and quivering lip, and knew not what to say, for he did not like to blame Sita herself unto her husband. On rushed Rama, torn with fear and self-reproach; they entered the cottage, and, behold! it was empty.

Then Rama turned more bitterly than before on Lakshman, and hard words passed between the brethren. Lakshman told his brother with what zeal he had assured Sita that Rama was proof against all the malice of fiends or men, and how it was only under her bitter taunts and shameful accusation that he had bent his will to leave her and go forth to carry aid. But Rama was ill pleased, and went forth with scant courtesy to look for traces of his wife. All round the cottage he searched in vain, loudly lamenting his fate, blaming his brother's faithlessness, accusing himself of some great sin that had brought such disaster upon him. Then, going farther afield, he called on birds and beasts, woods and fields, streams and mountains, sun, moon and stars, to reveal his lost Sita's whereabouts. In dread of Ravana, these gave him no clear word, but some pointed southward, and thither the brothers bent their steps. Then they came on scattered flowers, which Rama knew for Sita's; huge footprints were seen, and then came the marks of the strife with Jatayus—Ravana's broken bow, the wreck of his chariot, and Sita's ornaments lying around. Wildly raved Rama against the ravishers, and vowed destruction to the whole giant race, while Lakshman sought to curb his fury, showing how the footprints were those of one alone and not many. Then they came on the dying Jatayus, and Rama cried out that he, without doubt, had stolen and devoured Sita, and that he must perish forthwith. But the vulture found voice to say that his wounds were got in Sita's defence, and that the spoiler was Ravana. In great grief Rama fell down beside Jatayus, bewailing both his own misery and the woe he had brought on others. Then Jatayus feebly told them that Ravana had borne Sita away towards the south; with that he yielded up his breath, and the brothers performed his funeral ceremonies with much lamentation, and so went on their way.

Ere long they encountered a grim fiend named Kabandha, who attacked them fiercely, but was quickly laid low. As he lay dying, he asked who they were, and was filled with joy when he heard their names; for, he said, a curse had been laid on him by Indra, to pass from him only when he met with Rama and Lakshman. He bade them, therefore, burn his body, and he would then aid them with good counsel. Kabandha being dead, they laid his body on the funeral pyre, whence rose a goodly being, who mounted a car drawn by swans, and bade the princes seek out the monkey Sugriva, who dwelt by a certain lake. Sugriva, who was the son of Surya, the Sun-god, had been driven thither by his half-brother Bali, whose father was Indra.

The brethren therefore made their way through a fair country, rich in flowers and fruit, to the lotus-covered lake, nigh to which lived the monkey prince Sugriva. He, when he spied the noble pair approaching fully armed, was greatly troubled, supposing them to be sent for his destruction by Bali his brother. Removing, therefore, to another spot, he took counsel with his ministers, and sent forth Hanuman, son of the Wind-god, to take knowledge whether these were friends or foes.

So Hanuman, in the guise of a mendicant, went forth to meet the brothers, and bowing down before them, inquired in courteous and flattering terms who they were, whence they came, and what they would with Sugriva, whose land this was.

Rama was pleased with Hanuman's speech, which was delivered in the choicest language, giving proof of the finest training and study, and said that they sought Sugriva only for the benefit of his advice. This was good news to Hanuman, who joyfully foresaw that, with such allies as these, Sugriva would doubtless win back his kingdom. Learning more fully their story, he promised that Sugriva would help them to the best of his power; then, resuming his own giant form, he took the brethren up and bore them to Sugriva's presence.

The cause of the princes' coming having been explained, Sugriva offered them his hand in friendship. He then told Rama that, as he and four of his counsellors sat on a hill one day, a lady, borne through the sky by a fiend, had dropped her scarf and ornaments to them; and this had surely been Sita, in Ravana's grasp. The monkey prince then showed the tokens to Rama, who wept aloud, but was consoled and encouraged by Sugriva. The latter spoke of his own misfortune and misery, and declared how hope had come to him from the coming of Rama and Lakshman; these, therefore, might rest assured that their woes, in turn, would have a cheerful issue. Then Rama, being filled with new sympathy, asked of his fellow-sufferer the cause of Bali's enmity; on which Sugriva related the matter as follows:

"Bali is my elder brother, renowned for every kind of warlike prowess. To him I myself gave willing obeisance; and when the throne fell vacant, all chose him as king, and I gave full assent thereto. It chanced that strife for a woman's love arose betwixt my brother and a demon named Mayavi, son of Dundubhi—of whom more anon. This fiend came to Kishkindha, our capital, by night, and challenged Bali to the fray. Impetuous in his rage, my brother spurned all who sought to stay him, and, calling me to follow, rushed forth to combat. The fiend fled from the hot pursuit, and took refuge in a mighty cavern; my brother followed fiercely, bidding me to stay and watch the mouth of the cave under oath not to betray my trust. Long I waited patiently; then, at the end of a whole year, there rolled from the cave a frothing stream of gore. I listened for my brother's shout of triumph, but none came; whereon I, concluding that he had surely perished, closed the entrance of the cave with a huge rock and came away. On my return to Kishkindha, I told my tale and performed the funeral rites of him whom I supposed dead. Then the lords constrained me to be king in his place; so for a season I bare rule, methinks with justice. Then came Bali himself, joyful from the demon's slaughter, and found me king. In his rage he slew them that made me so, nor would any welcome of mine assuage his anger. He charged me with having barred the door of the cave to prevent his coming forth, while he pursued the demon in the far-off recesses of the cavern, so that I might win the kingdom for myself. My assurances, vows, and prayers, were all in vain. He believed me not, but drove me forth, to be as ye see me this day."

Then, in order to let Rama understand the tremendous power of Bali, Sugriva further related the tale of his brother's strife with Dundubhi, the father of Mayavi. This demon challenged the lord of Ocean to battle; but he declined, suggesting others who might fight; these, too, were unwilling, and in the end Bali was named as one likely to take up the challenge. So the demon, in the form of a monstrous buffalo, came to the gates of Kishkindha, and with menacing roars drew the attention of Bali. Nothing loth, the stalwart chief sallied forth, and, seizing the demon by the horns, flung him to the ground. Then, after a dreadful combat, he slew Dundubhi outright, and, snatching up the corpse, hurled it some miles away. Sugriva showed seven great trees which Bali, on this occasion, had pierced with one arrow; but Rama, with a single shaft, pierced not only the trees but also the hill beyond, the arrow then returning to the quiver. Seeing this, Sugriva was convinced that Rama was an ally whom even the celestials, led by Indra, could scarce withstand.

Sugriva then urged Rama to proceed at once against Bali. The two brother chieftains fought before the gates of Kishkindha, but Sugriva was worsted and reproached Rama for not helping him. To this Rama replied that they had been so closely intertwined that he had not dared to shoot; but that, if Sugriva hung a garland on his neck, he could be sure of shooting right. On this, Sugriva again went to Kishkindha with his friends, and with a savage roar challenged Bali to come forth. Bali's queen, Tara, strove to dissuade her lord from giving battle, for she was sure that Sugriva, once defeated, would not have returned to the fray unless he had got some puissant allies; but Bali was mad with rage, and would not hearken. In the duel that followed Sugriva again had the worse; but in the end Rama drew his bow and struck Bali to the heart. The dying chief reproached the prince for thus smiting him unawares; nor did Rama's reply, that Bali had wronged Sugriva by taking his kingdom and his wife, seem fairly to excuse him for smiting one engaged in single combat with another. Soon after, Bali died, asking his brother's pardon for his unkindness, and commending his son Angada to the care of Rama, who promised to befriend him loyally. Tara, Bali's widow, would not be comforted, and desired nothing better than to die on her husband's funeral pyre; but Rama calmed her and bade her live for the sake of Sugriva, from whom she had been taken, and of Angada her son. So after the funeral of Bali had been performed, Sugriva was installed as king with great pomp, and Tara again dwelt with him as queen.

During the rainy season, Rama and Lakshman lived in a cave on a hill not far distant. The beauty of the view and of the woods around them did much to charm their minds; but the thought of Sita was ever present to Rama, and Sugriva, now that his own end was gained, delayed his promised help. Restored to royalty and comfort, with Tara by his side, the monkey prince now gave himself more to pleasure than to affairs of state, and his debt to Rama remained unpaid and troubled him less and less as time went on. Rama complained to Lakshman that their ally, now freed from his own woes, gave little thought to the unchanged sorrows of his deliverer; and he bade his brother go to Kishkindha to remind Sugriva of the debt, lest, if he forgot

Rama's goodness, he might hear the twang of Rama's bow.

Readily and wrathfully Lakshman hastened to the city, and the monkeys fled before his presence Some of them bore tidings to Sugriva of Lakshman's advent; but the prince, absorbed in dalliance with Tara, gave the matter no heed. On this, Lakshman sent Angada to tell Sugriva of his waiting at the gate; but Sugriva was sunk in a drunken slumber. Then Lakshman came himself, and at his coming the monkeys roared so that Sugriva woke, and took advice of his counsellors, who advised him to return Lakshman a soft answer and to fulfil his promise to his benefactor Rama.

Replying to his ministers, Sugriva confessed that he had forgotten what was due to Rama, and prepared to meet Lakshman with folded hands. Thereon the hero was admitted, and, on entering the palace, was led to an inner chamber, where Sugriva sat on a richly dight throne. The monkey prince started up in terror as he heard Lakshman's threatening step, and awaited his coming in suppliant guise. Lakshman sternly reproved his base ingratitude, quoting to him words uttered of old by Brahma against the ungrateful:—

> "*For draughts of wine, for slaughtered cows,*
> *For treacherous theft, for broken vows,*
> *A pardon is ordained, but none*
> *For thankless scorn of service done.*"

In reply to this angry speech, Tara, the queen, interceded for Sugriva, and Lakshman's wrath was turned away. He confessed that, in his grief for

Rama, he had spoken more roughly than was needed; he acknowledged that Sugriva was not unworthy of the kingdom, and kindly feeling was thus restored.

Sugriva then carried Lakshman in his car back to Rama's presence, and stood before the prince with folded hands, promising at once to gather a mighty host, even millions and billions of monkeys. No sooner said than done; the monkey legions assembled in such numbers that the sun was darkened and the earth trembled. Then Rama desired that search should first be made to find where Sita was hidden.

Sugriva hereon appointed four armies to go forth and make search. The army of the East was led by Vinata; that of the West, by Sushena, Tara's father; Satabala commanded the Northern army, and Angada, with Hanuman and others, that of the South. Sugriva, who had ranged the whole world over to secure a safe refuge from Bali, gave them careful directions where to search. He looked with special hope to the southward army, for he greatly trusted Hanuman, who was strong and active as his sire, the Wind, and knew the Three Worlds perfectly.

This confidence, as has been well seen, was rightly placed. The armies of East, West, and North, after a month's constant searching, returned weary and despondent. And, indeed, for a time the army of Angada and Hanuman fared no better. They first ranged the mighty Vindhya mountains high and low, but no sign of Sita could they find. Then they passed through strange adventures in a wondrous cavern, out of which they were transported by magic to the shore of the sounding Ocean. Here dark despair came on them; the time of search was spent, and no trace or tidings of Sita had come to their ken. They dreaded the wrath of Sugriva, if they returned unsuccessful; and, doubting not that in such case he would slay them without pity, they determined to end their lives there by starvation.

In this sad plight they were succoured by Sampati, the elder brother of Jatayus, the giant vulture who had fought with Ravana to stay the rape of Sita. Sampati knew not of his brother's death, and heard the tale with deepest woe. But he had word of Sita for the seekers; for one day his son, who daily brought him food, had told him that he had heard of Ravana bearing her away; and Ravana dwelt in the splendid city of Lanka, girt with two hundred leagues of sea. Beyond all doubt, the wife of Rama must now be there.

This news filled Angada and Hanuman with joy, and they took counsel together how the belt of foaming sea might be passed. Many of the chiefs possessed great power of leaping; but the son of the Wind-god surpassed them all, for a leap of even a thousand leagues was no obstacle to him. So forth he sped, cheerfully vaunting his power to bound from one side of heaven to the other, and girt him for his leap across the strait.

So huge was the bulk of Hanuman that the mountain from which he sprang rocked beneath him as he leaped. Demons sought to stay his flight, but he rent and slew them. Then, shrinking to a lesser size lest the warders of Ravana's proud capital should mark his coming, he settled on a lofty peak, and thence made his way to the city, marvelling, as he went, at the goodly hills and rivers, the woods laden with flowers and fruit, and the plains rich in all manner of crops.

Entering the city, not without some pause, he surveyed its many marvels by the light of the clear full moon. The monkey prince saw with wonder broad streets, with goodly houses and palaces, some of seven or eight stories high, richly wrought of gold or dight therewith. Here also he saw the sleeping forms of many Rakshasas of every shape and size. Some were huge, others small; some were fair to look on, others vile and loathly; some bore wealth of rich jewels and raiment, others none at all. Greatly marvelling at everything, Hanuman wondered yet more when he came to the palace of the demon king, and most of all when he beheld, amid the many princely possessions therein, the Flower-car wrought by the architect of the gods, of which Ravana had bereft the lord of Wealth himself.

In this mansion Hanuman beheld Ravana himself asleep amid his wives, and he marvelled at their beauty; but though the fairest of them might well have rivalled Sita, Hanuman felt sure that Sita would ne'er be found among them, and he sought her elsewhere. Anon he came to a fair grove of lovely trees, broken by charming pools, clear as crystal and studded with blooming water-lilies. Here Hanuman saw a glistening white palace raised on a thousand pillars, with stairs of coral and pavement of gold. Here at last he found Sita, sweet as ever, but pale and wasted, like the dimly seen crescent of the new moon, or the Star-queen overborne by the tyranny of the planet Mars. Around the weeping queen stood a guard of fiendish dames, a grisly band; some had faces of beasts, some were hideous with every foul deformity, all were fierce and black of look, and all reeked of wine and blood.

As morning drew near Hanuman heard the sound of music and chanting, to greet the ears of the waking monarch. Up rose great Ravana then, and, with thoughts of captive Sita, arrayed himself with every care, and sought her presence once more. Desiring to note her bearing, Hanuman watched keenly from aloft.

Once more the demon king poured forth to Sita an impassioned prayer for her love; once more Sita, trembling and weeping, renounced the thought of being false to her lord. "Repent of thy sin," she cried, "and restore me to Rama. So shall it be well with thee; but otherwise, thou, thy city, and thy whole race are doomed to perish by his hand." He, thus repulsed, exchanged wooing for cursing, and vowed to have her life if he could not win her love. On his departure the Rakshasis, too, assailed her with cruel gibes and threats, scoffing at her folly in refusing the love of one who lorded it over gods and men. She, poor lady, like a fawn among wolves, sank trembling to the ground, wondering for what past sin she endured such torments.

At last they left her, and she sank to slumber. Then Hanuman debated in his heart how he might break his presence to Sita. "For," quoth he to himself, "if I speak in Sanskrit, the language of kings and Brahmans, she will think that Ravana addresses her; while if I use the vulgar tongue, she will yet think my apish form but a disguise of his. I will, therefore, gently rehearse in her hearing the tale of Rama's doings, and she will be soothed by the sound and praise of his name." Therewith he began softly to chant Rama's story, and she, greatly wondering, looked up and beheld him. Sore afraid at first, she doubted whether this were not a dream; but Hanuman drew near humbly, and told his errand. She, however, still fearing that this was in sooth none other than her deadly foe in disguise, would hold no parley with him for a space. This unbelief, he, in the end, o'ercame by telling her of Rama's appearance and virtues, and of his woe at her loss, and, lastly, by showing her the ring that Rama had given him as a token. She then told him that Ravana had given her two months to choose between his love and her own death; and giving him a jewel from her hair as a token, she charged him with her messages to Rama, and sent him forth with every good wish.

Yet would not Hanuman leave the fair city of Lanka without some mark of his enmity and his might. First he destroyed the pleasure-grove, uprooting the trees, marring the tanks, overthrowing the houses. Forth came the Rakshasa guards amain to stay the spoiler, but no easy task was theirs to deal with this strange foe. Having slain those who withstood him, he uprooted a huge pillar, and, whirling it round dashed it against the great temple of the Rakshasas, which took fire and was consumed. Other champions were then sent against him, but all in turn he overcame and slew. After these, Ravana bade his son Aksha engage Hanuman. Dread was the contest that ensued; and so great was the prowess of Aksha, that Hanuman, though superior in the fight, was fain to spare his life, but was constrained in the end to slay him. Another son of Ravana, Indrajit by name, mightier than his brother, then took up the gage of battle. Very puissant in fight was he, and Hanuman did rather avoid his strokes than seek to repay them. In the end, Indrajit brought forth a mystic weapon, whereby he noosed the monkey prince and took him prisoner; nor did Hanuman greatly grieve at this, for he was more than willing to be brought before Ravana and hold parley with him.

Full of wrath was the king when the prisoner was led into his presence, and, provoked by Hanuman's bold speech, was scarce restrained from causing him to be slain. Howbeit, in the end he gave order to set Hanuman free, as being an envoy; but he commanded that, in quital of Hanuman's doings, his tail should be set on fire ere he went. When this was done, Hanuman shrank in size till his bonds fell from him then he bounded aloft, and, waving his burning tail, set fire to the city, which burned amain. Ere he left Lanka, however, he once more had speech with Sita, comforting her with news of his success and with promise of Rama's coming to save her. Therewith he once more leaped the strait and rejoined his comrades.

VI

Overjoyed at Hanuman's return and tidings, Rama was yet much cast down concerning the crossing of the sea. He resolved, in any case, to march with all his host to the shore and there to take further counsel on the matter. Thither, accordingly, they made their way, and gazed with wonder on the surging sea, rife with many monsters huge and fierce.

Meanwhile, in Lanka, Ravana debated with his counsellors. Two to whom he gave special heed were his brothers Vibhishana and Kumbhakarna. Of these twain, Vibhishana had already chidden Ravana for the sin and folly of his doings, and even so he counselled him once more to give up Sita to her lord. "All has gone amiss," said he, "since thou didst bring her. Our realm has been o'ershadowed with evil and omens of ruin." But Ravana, enraged, started from his seat, and rushed forth to give charge concerning the defence of the city and the ordering of battle. Then he turned for advice to Kumbhakarna, who had just awaked from six months' sleep; for, though vast in bulk and of prodigious strength, he was given to gluttony and sloth.

Roused from his torpor, the giant mocked Ravana's hesitation. "Why vex thyself and us with these searchings of heart *now*, O King?" said he. "For such there was truly need, ere thy hand was laid on Sita. But now that she is indeed thy captive, there is no time for idle talk. Rouse thee! Be strong, fight, slay Rama! Thus only mayest thou win Sita's love. As for me, the first dart Rama hurls at me will be his last."

This counsel served but to vex the spirit of Ravana the more; for, in sooth, it would seem that, in spite of all his great boasting, he was in some measure cast down by the doings of Hanuman, and feared that, if the servant's deeds were so doughty, the master's stroke would be nothing less than deadly. But, impelled by fate, he spurned the advice of those who counselled the path of safety, and spake harshly to Vibhishana, saying that for such advice any other than he had surely died the death.

Then Vibhishana, weary of Ravana's pride and evil ways, took with him four attendants and fled across the sea to Rama's camp. Some, as he drew near, doubted his purpose; but Hanuman and Rama believed his words and welcomed him to their friendship. Then Rama, after hearing many things of Vibhishana, asked his advice concerning the passage of the strait, and was counselled to seek alliance with the lord of Ocean. Him, therefore, Rama entreated by prayer and sacrifice; but the lord of Ocean gave no sign. In the end, however, constrained by the prince's potent spells, he appeared, and bade Rama invoke the aid of Nala, son of the architect of the gods, to design a bridge across the foaming channel.

Then came Nala, rival of his father's skill, and under his eye the monkeys, in their thousands, cast into the sea rocks and timber without measure. Their ardour increased as the work advanced; and so zealously wrought they, that in no more than five days the two hundred leagues were spanned with a well-wrought causeway, and Rama and Lakshman, with the monkey leaders, led the many-millioned host in safety across to Lanka.

Ravana sent many spies to bring word of Rama's plans; all of these were captured in turn, but Rama treated them kindly and let them go. Then Ravana devised a cruel trick to bring Sita to despair. He called on one who had magic powers to make a head like that of a slaughtered man, even as the head of Rama slain, and weapons like his, stained with gore. Then he went once more to Sita to beg her love, telling how his men had surprised their foes in sleep, and one had cut off Rama's head and brought it together with his arms. When Sita gazed on the grisly trophies, she sank down like one dead; returning sense only brought overwhelming grief and the desire to be dead with him who had thus died for her.

Then came one seeking Ravana on urgent business, and he went forth to direct the ordering of his host. When he was gone, a Rakshasi, kindlier than the rest, bade her be of good cheer, for this tale of the head was but a trick of art magic; Rama lived, and it was the instant call to prepare for battle with him that had drawn Ravana forth. As she spake, the earth shook and the air resounded with the noise of warlike preparation; and Sita was comforted by her companion's words, as parched ground by rain.

Meanwhile Rama and Lakshman, with Sugriva and Vibhishana, having taken counsel for the attack on the city, passed the night on a fair hill whence a goodly view of Lanka spread itself before their eyes. On the morrow Sugriva, beholding Ravana sitting in state on a tower over the gateway, could hold himself no longer, but sprang over the space between and, bounding at the demon king, with loud threat attacked him forthwith. Ravana was not slow to resist, and

Sugriva, having somewhat the worse of the encounter, escaped to his friends.

The monkeys now advanced to the assault in millions, and Ravana from his watch-tower beheld the earth tawny with their bodies. A furious battle raged all day, with many single combats between the leaders on either part. Rama wrought dire havoc among the Rakshasas; but young Indrajit, coming fiercely to the fray, bound both him and Lakshman with a magic noose and rained hissing shafts upon them amain. Their strength failed, and with dimmed eyes they sank to earth. Loud shouted Indrajit in triumph, and loud yelled the fiends on every side, and deep woe came on Sugriva and his friends. Ravana, rejoicing, sent word to Sita that the heroes were fallen, and she was taken in a car to the place where they lay. Breaking out into wild lament, she cried, "False were the soothsayers who foretold that I should be a mother and never a widow; false, they who said I should reign as Rama's queen. Slain is he now, my lord and life, matchless in might—he who, with unaided arm, o'erthrew the fiends sent against us in the forest—slain by base illusion, who ne'er could have been worsted in fair fight. Alas for me! Alas, still more, for the widowed mother who, with bowed head, counts days and hours to his return whom she ne'er again will see!"

Then Rama, waking weakly from the trance that held him, saw his brother lying as dead, and made sore lament; his hope of ruling in Lanka seemed blasted, and he woefully bade Sugriva give up the struggle and return to his kingdom.

Then, while some sought to hearten Rama, and others talked of bringing leaves of healing from the shore of the Milky Ocean, there gathered, as it were, a sudden storm all round. Loud blew the blast, and fierce flashed the lightning; trees were uprooted, the hills were riven, the waters feared and foamed. On this blast came Garuda, king of birds, the steed of Vishnu, the foe of serpents, amid flames of light. At the glance of his fiery eye, the serpent bond that held the princes was loosed in a twinkling; at the touch of his wing, their pangs were allayed and their bodies made every whit whole. Then up they stood rejoicing, and thanked their healer, not knowing who he was. Then answered Garuda, with pride and joy, "Know me for one who loved thee of old, O Rama! I am Garuda, lord of all that fly. These snares, that bound thee and thy brother, were, in sooth, none other than mighty snakes, and among all the celestials none could loose them save myself, the foe of serpents. On then, in this thy strength renewed, and smite the foe of gods and men!" Thus spake Garuda, and, swift as thought, sped skyward in a blaze of light.

Learning that the princes had been loosed from their bonds, Ravana was greatly troubled, but gave command for a sally by some of his best warriors; when these were slain, he went forth himself. Many of the monkey chiefs he slew or drove wounded from the fight, but Rama and Lakshman withstood him. Lakshman was borne from the field, stricken and senseless, by Hanuman; but Ravana's might failed before Rama, and he withdrew to the city, abashed and defeated. In this despondent mood, he commanded that Kumbhakarna should be waked from his renewed slumber. Vast store of meat and wine was taken to be ready for the giant glutton on his rousing; then was he stirred from sleep, yet so only with great toil, nor did his slumber yield until he had been trampled by elephants. Then, after fiercely asking wherefore they had roused him, he gorged himself with food and sought Ravana's presence.

The downcast king beheld with lightened cheer his brother's monstrous form, and Kumbhakarna heartened him with stout words of his own prowess. Then the huge champion went forth to battle and wrought havoc in the ranks of his foes. Many a grim encounter he had with their chiefs, but none made head against him, till he called on Rama to fight hand to hand. Even Rama's weapons failed to daunt the giant, till, with the dart bearing Indra's name, the prince shore off an arm, and then both legs. Then with a final blow Kumbhakarna's head was smitten off, and his maimed body fell crashing into the sea.

The sons of Ravana with difficulty dispelled their father's overwhelming grief and alarm at the defeat and death of his puissant brother. Themselves doughty warriors, they went forth with high courage to avenge Kumbhakarna's death. But one and all fell. Angada slew one; Lakshman, another; other twain perished before the valour of Hanuman.

There remained, however, one both mighty of arm and skilled in cunning devices, whose prowess had already well-nigh wrought the heroes' bane.

Indrajit sallied forth anew, boiling with rage and before his wild onslaught the monkeys fell in myriads, and Sugriva, Hanuman, and other chiefs were driven wounded from the fray. Again on Rama and Lakshman fell the magic noose, inevitable, numbing all their powers, so that they sank as dead. But Hanuman sped swiftly to the mountains of the North, and there from a noble hill he culled and brought four herbs of healing, whereby the heroes were loosed and quickened and new virtue was imparted to all the host.

Thereafter Indrajit gave himself anew to magical practice, seeking to render himself invisible and proof against every wound. Also, he brought forth a likeness of Sita, pale and worn, and slew the same in sight of Hanuman. He, in turn, carried the dreadful news to Rama, whose soul fainted at the tidings Then Lakshman was bidden to go forth in haste, to do battle against Indrajit, ere that warrior should complete the spells rendering him invulnerable. Lakshman, therefore, sought the sacred ground where Indrajit wrought his magic, and called on him to fight. As may be supposed, the combat was one of the most close and bitter of all the many that were fought; but Lakshman, though sorely wounded, prevailed in the end, and great Indrajit was slain.

There remained nothing now for Ravana but to take the field himself and to bide there till victory or death. The battle now raged with unmeasured fury, with many fierce encounters between the captains and infinite slaughter of the common sort. Then Vibhishana arose against his brother and did battle with him who was the chief of his own blood

"Rama launched at his Foe a fearsome Bolt"

and race. In this emprise he came nigh to being slain, but he was saved once by Rama and again by Lakshman. The Rakshasa king, mad with rage against his brother, cried out that Lakshman interfered thus to his own hurt; and indeed the great spear of Ravana smote the rescuer and laid him low. But again Hanuman sped to Himalaya for healing herbs, and therewith Lakshman was saved from death.

Then Rama, burning for vengeance, made ready for battle, and Indra lent him his car and heavenly charioteer. But Ravana slew the god's steeds and well-nigh wrecked the car; whereat the gods trembled and the sun hid his face. Howbeit, Rama dealt Ravana a grievous wound, and after further conflict the demon king was brought so low, that none too soon his charioteer bore him away from the fray. But, recovering, he addressed himself once more to the fight.

Rama, too, having worshipped the Sun, the dispeller of darkness, the all-beholding, with Vedic hymns, drove to meet the foe with all confidence. For seven days and nights the awful duel continued. Rama cut off one or more of the ten heads of Ravana, not once but many times; but the heads grew afresh from the wounds, and the giant fought on undismayed.

Then at last Rama launched at his foe a fearsome bolt forged for Indra at Brahma's behest, winged with the wind and tipped with the sun's fire.

> "*And swift the limb-dividing dart*
> *Pierced the huge chest and cleft the heart;*
> *And dead he fell upon the plain,*
> *Like Vritra by the Thunderer slain.*"

Amid all the plaudits of men, saints and gods, that greeted the crowning success of Rama's warfare, there was one among his following whose heart was sore for the fallen king. Sadly Vibhishana bent o'er the corpse, and thus, lamenting, he spake, "Alas, hero, valiant and skilful in fight, why liest thou low on thy gory bed? Thy fate has been even as I foreboded; but love and pride forbade thee listen to my friendly counsel. Alas for the pride of the Rakshasa race, once a tree of royal growth and stature, now lying prostrate,

"*With rifled bloom and mangled bough.*"

Him Rama, the joyous victor himself, did kindly console. "Weep not," he said, "for the intrepid king who died a warrior's death. Hatred between us perishes with his fall, and I shall gladly aid thee to perform the last duties in his honour."

Vibhishana feared somewhat to essay funeral rites on behalf of one so evil as Ravana had been; but Rama bade him believe that there should be no enmity towards the dead, and all was therefore duly made ready and carried out.

Then Rama, returning to the camp, gave out his wish that Vibhishana should be made king in Ravana's place. The anointing water was speedily brought from Ocean in a golden jar, and Rama sprinkled the head of Vibhishana, as the new lord of Lanka, in presence of the Rakshasas; and all were glad.

Then Rama bade Hanuman go bear tidings to Sita. Her the monkey prince found, still sad and poorly arrayed, sitting 'neath a tree, surrounded by her

Rakshasi guards. Right welcome to her was the sight of Hanuman, but the joy of his tidings at first reft her of speech. Anon she talked with him for a space; then suffered him to depart, with the message that she craved sight of her lord. Then Rama sent her word to deck herself and come, which forthwith she did; but the crowd so pressed to see her, that Vibhishana and others drove them back. This vexed Rama, who said that this was not a time at which a wife need shrink from showing her face.

Further, when, somewhat daunted by these words, Sita drew near humbly and stood at Rama's side, he greeted her with little warmth, saying, "Lady, the insult is avenged, the task is done. These, whom thou seest, have battled successfully; the blot on mine honour is avenged." Tears came to Sita's eyes at this chill welcome; but Rama, no whit melted, spake again, yet more cruelly, saying, "'Twas not for love of thee that I dared this deed, but to avenge mine honour. Thou hast been embraced by Ravana's arm, thou hast been the inmate of his palace. 'Twere better thou shouldest go free. Duty bids me speak thus: thou art free to go where thou wilt."

Amazed and shame-stricken by these cutting words, Sita, trembling like a creeper rent by an elephant, pleaded woefully with her husband to say what cause he had to distrust her, and why he had not sent word of his jealousy by Hanuman. Then, turning to Lakshman, she said in broken accents, "Prepare for me, son of Sumitra, the funeral pyre! Disowned and shamed, I cannot bear to live."

Nor did Rama gainsay this baleful request. All in

his sight and hearing the pile was prepared, and Sita essayed to step into the blazing fire. Ere she did so, she called on the Fire, the purifier of all things, to witness that she had never in thought or word or deed swerved from loyal love to her lord. Then with unfaltering step she passed into the flame; and a piercing cry of anguish broke from all, as they saw her fall in its fierce embrace.

Then the god of Fire rose from the midst of the pile, leading Sita forth, witnessing to Rama that neither by thought nor by word nor by deed had she turned from her loyalty to him. The gods, too, had come themselves to chide Rama for suffering his faithful wife to enter the fire. To these protests he made answer that he had never really doubted his Sita's truth, but had merely put her to the test that all might see the matter publicly righted and know him for an honourable man.

Yet, in sooth, this bearing of Rama towards his wife seems scarce that of kindness or true honour. Better had it been for him, even in the face of slander—though never a word thereof had gone abroad—to believe his most true and loving wife and to cleave to her through good report and bad. Braver, surely, to have calmly taken her hand in his and so stood side by side with her against the sneers of men—though of these there were none. And, indeed, if she was constrained to feel the insulting touch of Ravana's arm on her waist, and to sojourn, a weeping captive, in the chambers of his palace, the fault was surely Rama's own. The weakness for which he so bitterly chid his brother, in respect of leaving her side to satisfy her timid yearning for

"The God of Fire rose from the midst"

her husband's safety, had been shown by himself when, yielding his better judgment to her plea, he began the movement which left her defenceless, by going forth to chase the magic deer.

Yet the lesson is one that, alas, is true to the nature of mortal men. For while trouble is heavy on us, we are ever ready to share the burden of those who are caught in the same toils as ourselves; but when the cloud of care rolls by, and the crushing load of sorrow grows lighter, we begin to cast the eye of judgment on our fellows, and to think that our falling into the pit was of their doing, though, haply, they might with greater justice say the like of us.

Be this as it may, husband and wife were now happily joined together again. Then came one of the great gods, Siva, having in his car Dasaratha, Rama's sire, and greeted the conquering hero. "Go back to thy kingdom now," said the departed monarch, "the fourteen years are ended, and thy mother awaits thee."

Thereon Vibhishana brough forth the Flower-car, won of old by Ravana from the lord of Wealth, to convey Rama and his queen to Ayodhya. Wondrous to behold was this divine chariot, all decked with gold; it was huge of size, and had goodly chambers within; bells hung around it and tinkled as it moved; also it was drawn by bright swans, and fared whithersoever those within it willed.

Sweetly passed the homeward journey, as each to other recounted the strange adventures that had passed upon them in the days of their separation. By Sita's request, Rama's staunch allies, the monkey lords, were invited to follow and be present in Ayodhya when the prince should be enthroned.

Before the royal pair sped Hanuman, bearing word of their coming to Bharat. That faithful regent still dwelt humbly at Nandigrama; in hermit guise he passed his days, his brother's sandals ever set up in his view. Forthwith, on hearing the joyful tidings, he bade men level the roads and strew them with flowers; musicians and trumpeters made merry din, and so great was the joyous clamour on every side that beneath them the earth shook withal. Then came Rama from the hermitage where erst he had stayed on his way to the forest, and was received humbly by Bharata, who placed the sandals at his feet, blessing the day that witnessed the return of Ayodhya's rightful lord. Thereon Rama, now restored to his native land, gave command that the Flower-car should be sent back to the god of Wealth, from whom Ravana of yore had stolen it; and, receiving back the kingdom, was installed with Sita on a jewelled throne, and so anointed king by the hands of holy sages, with water brought from many holy streams.

The Wind-god, sire of Hanuman, gave to Rama a wreath of golden lotuses, to crown him withal; water-nymphs danced a fairy measure, while storm-sprites and heavenly minstrels swelled the jocund strain of praise. Glorious gifts were bestowed on the princes who had befriended Rama so loyally, and all returned homeward in supreme content.

Of the latter end of Rama and Sita, and how they passed from among the children of men, the tale need not here be told. Sufficient be it to leave them, joined together after such grievous parting, and gloriously enthroned after such unseemly abasement, to reign over their rejoicing realm in peace and prosperity for many a hundred year.

> "*Ten thousand years Ayodhya, blest*
> *With Rama's rule, had peace and rest.*
> *No widow mourned her murdered mate,*
> *No house was ever desolate.*
> *The happy land no murrain knew,*
> *The flocks and herds increased and grew.*
> *The earth her kindly fruits supplied,*
> *No harvest failed, no children died.*
> *Unknown were want, disease, and crime:*
> *So calm, so happy was the time.*"

The verses in this Tale are quoted by the kind permission of the publishers Messrs. Trübner, Kegan, Paul and Co., from the verse translation (1870) of Valmiki's "Ramayana," by R. T. H. Griffith.

Chapter III

THE TALE OF PRAHLADA, THE GOOD DANAVA

IN far distant ages there lived on earth a mighty Danava, Hiranyakasipu by name, son of Diti, the old Earth-mother, whose progeny were also called Daityas, after her own name.

This Danava lord had won from the Creator a mystic boon, through the strength of which he had come to hold sway over all three worlds. The celestials trembled before his might, as they did before that of Ravana, of whom we read elsewhere. In truth, this Danava was none other than Ravana himself, in an earlier existence ; and like Ravana he loved not righteousness, but hated the gods and all that tended to their honour.

Hiranyakasipu had gotten to himself the control of sun and moon and all the host of heaven, the lordship over wealth, and the judgment of the dead. Nagas and Gandharvas did fealty to him, and attended his presence ; at his banquets the perfected saints sang praises, and nymphs of heaven danced thereto. Thus the Daitya king was mightily puffed up with pride, and the gods fled abashed before him, and hid themselves in mortal guise.

A son he had, Prahlada by name, a youth of wondrous wisdom and goodness. Him the king committed to the charge of his priests, to be instructed in all useful learning and matter of kingcraft. And in time it chanced that Hiranyakasipu called for the lad, and bade him tell what he had learned of his teachers. To this the youth replied:

"I have learned to adore him who is the Cause of causes, even Vishnu, the imperishable lord of the Universe."

Then was his father filled with fury, for no name was so hateful to him as that of Vishnu; and in hot anger he cried aloud to the priest:

"What meanest thou, wretch, thus to teach my son to flout me by praising to my very face him whom I hate above all others?"

Then answered the priest gravely, that what Prahlada said had not been taught by himself. "By whom, then?" asked the king.

Then spake Prahlada himself and said, "Who should teach me such knowledge but he who is the supreme Teacher, indwelling the hearts of all who will learn of him? Vishnu himself, dwelling in my heart, has taught me."

Then was Hiranyakasipu yet more wroth, and cried, "Who is Vishnu, and what is he to thee, that thou laudest him thus before me, ruler of the three worlds?"

"Vishnu," replied the youth," is the Lord of all the Universe, not only of me, but of thee, father, also. He by his divine power ruleth over all, even over thyself; why, then, shouldest thou be offended at his praise?"

"Away with the young fool!" cried the king wildly. "Let him return to his lessons and learn wisdom. Whence learns he thus profanely to extol my worst foe?"

So Prahlada returned to the house of his preceptor; and there, by diligence and devotion, throve apace in all manner of religious knowledge. After certain days, his father summoned him again, and bade him recite some poem. Thereon the youth opened, after the manner of poets, with invocation of a god, and the god whose favour he invoked was Vishnu. His father, beside himself with rage, bade the attendants fall on his son and smite him, as a traitor to his friends and a curse to all his race. This the Danavas did, smiting the lad grievously and often. But he, meditating on Vishnu, felt no pain from their blows; and when his father promised him relief, if he would but take back his praise of Vishnu, he answered that he, in whose heart dwelt the immortal guardian from all the woes of existence, knew no need of relief.

Then Hiranyakasipu, in his wrath and indignation, called on the Nagas, the snake-gods, to slay his son with their venom; and the Naga lords bit him in every part with their deadly fangs. But he, absorbed in rapture of devotion, felt no pain nor suffered scathe; while they, the serpent-lords, cried out, "O king, our fangs are broken, our crests are burst, we are racked with fever; but the youth is unscathed, and thou must seek other aid."

Then the king summoned the celestial elephants,

Prahlada overcoming the Elephants

huge as mountains, to trample and gore his son to death; and this, indeed, they strove to do. But Prahlada, thus fearfully assailed, cried out, "The tusks of the elephants are blunted on my body: and this through no strength of mine but through meditation on Vishnu, who preserveth from all affliction."

Then cried the king, "Away with the elephants, and let fire consume the rebel!" So the Danavas piled great heaps of wood around Prahlada, and kindled the same; and the wind, at the king's command, fanned the flame to exceeding great heat. But even so the youth cried to his father, "The flame, though fanned by the wind, doth not burn me, but all around me seems cool and fragrant, as the open air amid beds of flowers."

Then drew near the king's priests, illustrious and learned Brahmans, saying, "O king, let not thine anger wax hot against the lad! Youth is the season of error, and it becomes thee not to be bitter against thy son. Commit him to our care, and we shall patiently instruct him to labour for the ruin of thy foes. Howbeit, if he still continue in his devotion to Vishnu, we shall then compass his death by unfailing means.

Thus persuaded, the Daitya king once more committed Prahlada to his preceptor's keeping. But in this estate, the prince, never idle, betook himself to imparting the lore of Vishnu to the young Daityas. "Set not your hearts," said he, "on things of time and sense. To birth, growth, and maturity, succeeded inevitable decay and death; and attachment to the pleasure of this life breeds but sorrow and anguish when time bids us part with that which we have loved too well. Thus do men in youth give themselves wholly to pleasure; and when middle age and decay come upon them, behold, they are ignorant and weak, nor have they longer the power to perform those duties which should have been their care in earlier years. In this ocean of sorrow and perplexity, let Vishnu be your refuge. Let not one who is fortunate boast himself over one who is not, nor let him who suffers affliction envy him who lives at ease; for the suppression of ill-feeling on either side is the only true happiness for each, and is in itself the greatest reward. Think not to obtain lasting satisfaction from the chances and changes of life; but know that by devotion to Vishnu alone can true peace and happiness be obtained. Such bliss neither man nor beast, neither monster nor demi-god can dispel—and fair will be the fruit that ye gather from the never-failing tree of wisdom."

Such was the goodly discourse of Prahlada to the Daitya youths of his generation. But some of these, fearing the wrath of the king, reported the matter. Thereon Hiranyakasipu, greatly incensed, sent for his cooks and said, "The vile wretch, my son, seeks to destroy the souls of others with his hateful doctrine; make haste, therefore, and mix baleful drugs with all his food, and cause him to perish without delay."

So the cooks mixed fell poison with all that should be set before Prahlada, and he ate thereof according to his wont. And, by reason of his meditating ever on the Eternal One, the deadly poison became harmless within him, and he digested all without scathe. So the cooks told it to the king.

Then Hiranyakasipu called for his priests, and bade them instantly perform mystic rites that should cause his son's death. So they stood before the youth, and, having chanted hymns of the Veda, said to him, "Thou, O prince, art born in the family of the Daitya king, who is lord of the three worlds: what owest thou to the gods, and why seekest thou to lean on the Eternal? Thy sire is lord of the three worlds, and so in turn shalt thou be. Thy father merits thy worship before all; desist, then, from praising his deadly enemy."

To them answered Prahlada, "Noble Brahmans, rightly indeed do ye speak of the reverence due to a father; rightly do we extol the greatness of our race; and rightly, too, would ye remind me that this my father bears rule over the three worlds. In all these things, I gainsay you nought; but when ye bid me have no dependence on the Eternal, your words are but foolishness." Therewith he kept silence for a space, lest he should seem to mock those worthy of his respect. But anon the smiles brake forth on his face, and he cried, "What need to lean on the Eternal, forsooth! A goodly question, indeed, most worthy of such venerable preceptors! If it be indeed in good faith that ye ask, then must I needs instruct you touching dependence on the Eternal. Is he, from whom come the four ends of man—virtue, desire, wealth, and final salvation—of no account? All that is good for men cometh through the glorification of Vishnu; how then ask ye, 'What need of the Eternal?' Yet, enough of speech;

ye are my preceptors; speak ye as seemeth you right, for the matter resteth not on my weak judgment."

Then answered the priests, "Boy, we sought aforetime to preserve thee, not knowing the depth of thy folly. Now, however, if thou change not thy speech, we shall forthwith essay rites that will surely cause thy death."

But Prahlada replied, "What mean ye by death? For know that true death is wrought by none save oneself, as one follows evil or good."

Then by their magic rites, the Daitya priests brought forth a fearsome female form, all dight with fiery flame, parching the earth beneath her tread; and she, approaching the prince, smote him on the breast with a fiery trident. But that breast, indwelt by the imperishable Lord, would have turned a thunderbolt; and the magic weapon shivered into a hundred pieces. Then the dread being, foiled in her attack, turned on those who had raised her, and destroyed them. But Prahlada, seeing their end, called on the Imperishable, saying, "O Thou, who art everywhere present and all-powerful, preserve these Brahmans from the destroying fire! If my heart is truly free from malice toward my foes, then let these be restored to life! If through devotion to thee, I have felt no unkindness toward those who would have poisoned me, the elephants that would have crushed me, and all others that sought my life: then, I pray Thee, let these Daitya priests live again!"

Then, in answer to his prayer, the priests rose up, uninjured and rejoicing; and, having blessed the prince and wished him all prosperity, they departed to the king of the Daityas and told him all that had passed. So, when Hiranyakasipu heard that the priestly enchantments had failed, he sent for his son and sought to know the secret of his might.

"Whence, Prahlada," he said, "come these wondrous powers of thine? Are they born of magic, or have they been thine since birth?"

"Whate'er I possess," his son replied, "is neither mine own by nature nor magic-born; it is the portion of all alike in whose hearts the Blessed One abides. I see Him in all around me, and I cherish no malice against any; and them who are thus fortified neither bodily nor mental pain, whether by gods or men inflicted, can in any wise hurt."

Dark lowered the brow of the Daitya king at these words, and he bade the attendants seize his son and hurl him from the summit of his palace, many leagues in height, on to the mountain crags. So down they flung him; but he, cherishing Vishnu in his heart, fell softly, and Earth, the nurse of all creatures, gathered him softly to her lap.

Seeing the lad thus uninjured and every whit whole, Hiranyakasipu betook himself to Sambara, the great enchanter; who bade the king be sure that by some device he would swiftly compass Prahlada's bane. Then the vain demon practised sundry wiles against the prince; but by his constant meditation on the Lord of all, every wile was brought to nought. Then the king summoned the wind to blow upon and blast his son; and the wind blew, cold, cutting, insufferable. It pierced right into the lad's frame; but the mighty upholder of all things, enthroned within the prince's heart, waxed wroth, and drank up the evil wind and rendered it of none effect.

Thus foiled in his murderous intent, the king abated somewhat of his purpose, and sent his son back to his preceptor's house. Here his teacher instructed him with all diligence, and anon told the king that the prince was now well versed in all the science of kingcraft. So Hiranyakasipu called Prahlada, and asked him divers questions touching the duty of kings; as, how to handle affairs at periods of advance, stagnation, or falling away; with whom to form alliances; how to vanquish forest and mountain tribes; and many other such things. To all this, Prahlada replied, "It is true, O father, that all these things have been taught me, and I have learned them dutifully; but I approve not all that I have learned. For herein there is much concerning the conquest of foes and the gaining of friends; but, whereas I know neither friend nor foe, whereto serveth all this instruction for me? That which tendeth to deliverance from bondage is the true knowledge; all else is but idle cleverness. And concerning this true knowledge, I may yet more fully speak. He who, in this life, covets neither dominion nor wealth, shall assuredly obtain both in the life to come. Many go to and fro, toiling to be great; but greatness consisteth not in the position, but in the character of him who gains it. High estate is often granted by fate to fools and cowards, but true greatness and final bliss are the portion of him who looks on all with equal charity and is assiduous in the practice of virtue. Such an one sees Vishnu in all the Universe around him; and with such knowledge the Eternal is well pleased."

Then, transported with rage, the Daitya king sprang from his throne, and, spurning Prahlada with his foot, cried to his myrmidons, "Ho, thou! and thou! seize him and bind him, and cast him forthwith into the ocean, lest all our race be corrupted with his vile teaching. Though oft forbidden, he will in no wise cease from uttering the praises of my mortal foe."

So they bound him fast, and flung him into the sea, which was straightway mightily convulsed, and heaved amain, as though to overflow the world. Beholding his son float safely on the waters, the king called on his folk to rain great rocks upon the prince, so that, if he would not die, he must needs live only beneath the close-piled rocks, pressed down to ocean's bed. So the Danayas hurled on Prahlada huge masses of rock, and piled them thick upon him so that he lay beneath miles of rock at the bottom of the sea. But, thus lying, he fixed his heart constantly on Vishnu, the Soul of all, and with manifold utterance gave voice to his praise. Thus constantly meditating on the Lord of all creatures, he felt himself united with the divine spirit; the imperishable Vishnu, whose being is all wisdom, became present in his soul, and he was purified from all stain. Then, with this consciousness of Vishnu's indwelling, his bonds were burst asunder; the ocean was troubled and heaved violently; all the denizens of the vast deep trembled; earth with all its mountains quaked exceedingly; and the prince, putting aside the rocky masses piled on him, came forth from the depths.

When he again saw the outer world around him, and knew himself once more restored to ordinary being, he opened his lips anew in praise to Vishnu, the soul and life of all things, glorified for ever. Thereon, the god himself appeared visibly before him, clad in yellow robes; and when Prahlada had saluted him with all reverence, bade him choose some boon. To this answered Prahlada, "In all the various existences through which my soul may be doomed to pass, may I never be moved from fixed devotion to thee, O Blessed One!"

"This," replied Vishnu, "thou hast by thy constant meditation already gained for thyself, and needest not to ask it. Demand another boon."

Then said the prince, "My father, alas, has wrought much evil against me, and has compassed my death in many ways—by poison, by snake-bite, by the goring of elephants, by grievous enchantments, and other means. As, by thy mercy and through faith in thee, I have passed through all unharmed, so grant unto him forgiveness for all."

"Be it granted, even as thou askest," said the god; "yet I grant thee another boon—ask, therefore, O Daitya prince!"

Then answered the youth, "Nought need I ask, since in thee I have all that heart can wish. Wealth, prosperity, and merit are of no account unto me now; for him whose heart is fixed on thee is free from all need."

So Vishnu blessed him and vanished from his sight; and the young man returned to his father, and saluted him, and told what had passed. Then his father was moved to repentance, and embraced his son and treated him kindly; and Prahlada, while his father lived, ever bore him due reverence and in all things served him.

Concerning the end of Hiranyakasipu, however, there is but one tale: to wit, that he perished under the wrath of Vishnu, who appeared for that purpose in the guise of a monster, half man and half lion. And some records aver that the king's quarrel with his son endured to the end, and that it was this quarrel that led to the father's destruction. For, they say, Hiranyakasipu, disputing his son's statement that Vishnu was present everywhere and in everything, demanded to know whether Vishnu were present in a certain great pillar of his hall, and therewith smote the pillar vehemently. Whereon the monstrous Man-lion issued from the pillar itself and rent the Daitya king in pieces.

However this may be, Prahlada succeeded his sire in the kingdom, and ruled over the Daityas for many years with that prosperity which is held to be the proper fruit of devotion to duty and to the welfare of one's subjects.

Chapter IV

THE TALE OF KUVALAYASWA

THERE lived once a noble monarch, named Satrujit, that is, "conqueror of his foes," as in truth he was; and he had a son named Ritudhwaja, who was in every way worthy of such a father, being victorious in war and eminent alike in power of mind and in beauty of person.

This prince lived a life rich in study as well as in the pursuit of pleasure. At one time he would give himself to mastering the sacred scriptures, or to studying the science of war in all its branches; at others, he drank the joys of poetry, singing, drama, and dicing, and disported himself in the practice of every kind of weapon. In these various pursuits he enjoyed the companionship of many young princes, his equals in the warrior caste; while youthful Brahmans also, and the noblest of those of lower degree, found a welcome with the king's son.

Then it came to pass that two young Nagas, sons of Aswatara, a noble prince among the snake-gods, came from the lower regions to visit the world of men; and, assuming the guise of Brahman youths, they too entered the company of Ritudhwaja, and with him passed many days in all sorts of gay employ. Day by day the friendship betwixt the prince and the two young Nagas grew apace; they were joined to him by ties of close affection, while he knew no pleasure apart from them, neither eating nor drinking nor bathing, nor any sort of pleasurable or strenuous exercise. Thus passed the days; the nights, the two Nagas spent in Patala, sighing for the dawn of day to suffer them to seek again the prince's company.

Then, one day, their father inquired of them, saying, "Tell me, dear sons, with whom in the upper world are ye joined in such close affection?"

Then the twain, doing obeisance to their father, answered, "It is the son of King Satrujit that draws us thither; a noble and upright hero is he, kindly, learned, handsome in person, the foe of all that is dishonourable, and a very mine of all that is virtuous. So yearn our hearts for him, that thus separate we take little delight in this our home; the Naga world seems chill and comfortless, while above ground his company and the sun's glad rays combined to warm and cheer us. To them answered their father:

"Happy son of holy sire must he be, in sooth, whom such as yourselves praise so devotedly even in his absence! There are evil men learned in the Scriptures, and good men who are fools; but truly estimable is he who is both good-hearted and learned in sacred lore. His father's pride is that son whose friends praise his goodness and whose enemies confess his valour. As to this noble youth, I doubt not but he has been your benefactor in some matter—happy is he who is both ready and able to meet the petitions of his friends! Whatever in this house, of wealth or living things, might please the prince, that let him have with all good will! Shame on us, if, having received bountifully, we make no return for these benefits!"

To this the king's sons answered and said, "But what, O father, can we find here that this highly-favoured prince lacks? The like of his jewels is not to be seen in Patala; such also are his ornaments and clothing, his steeds and chariots. As for his knowledge, he is without peer, and even to the wise he is as an oracle. And in the matter of achievement, he has wrought an exploit so marvellous that it might be wrought by scarcely any save Brahma, Vishnu, Siva, or the other gods."

Then the Naga lord Aswatara, moved by curiosity, bade his sons tell the tale of their comrade's exploit. "For," quoth he, "the man of steadfast spirit may attain even to the position of a god, or any other high estate. To those who have the mastery of their own spirits and are constant in their purpose, there is little or nought that is truly impossible. Behold how far removed from earth is the Pole Star! Yet did a mortal prince, a denizen of earth, attain thereto and became its lord. Relate, then, the adventure of your friend, my sons."

Now, though this matter of the mortal prince and the Pole Star scarce belongs to this tale itself, yet it is in any case worth telling; and as it is here mentioned, it may find a place not unworthily forthwith.

The Story of Dhruva.

There lived of yore a king named Uttanapada, who had two wives, Sûniti and Suruchi by name; and of these, Suruchi was the favourite. A son was born to her, named Uttama, and to Suniti one named Dhruva.

When these children were somewhat grown, it chanced on a day that King Uttanapada dandled Suruchi's son upon his knee; seeing which, the five-year-old Dhruva was fain to climb up too; but the king did not even notice him. Thereon Suruchi, seeing the despised wife's son thus slighted, spake arrogantly to the child in the king's hearing, saying, "Thou art unfit for such honour—why seek it? If thou wouldst have it, go, adore the Supreme Being!"

Struck by these harsh words, the child Dhruva, sighing like a snake hissing in anger, left his father and repaired to his mother; and she, racked with grief, like a creeper caught in a forest fire, wept copiously. Then she said, "What my rival wife has said, is true: it is only by adoring the Supreme Being that thou canst overcome this inferiority."

With that, the boy, collecting his spirits, left his father's house, to do that which had been told him; and as he went, he met the sage Narada, who laid his hands upon him and blessed him, saying, "Surely thou art too young to vex thy spirit with thoughts of honour and dishonour; but if such thoughts do trouble thee, rest assured that the Deity overrules all actions. As for thy purpose, that

One whom thou seekest is exceeding hard to approach. Even ascetics, who renounce all, hardly attain thereto in many births. One should be content with destiny; for contentment brings salvation. He who reveres his superiors, is kind to those beneath him, and loves his equals, need have no regrets."

Then answered Dhruva, "True it may be that only such as thou namest are likely to attain this object; but I come of warrior stock, and Suruchi's words have riven my heart. I have resolved to surpass all that has ever been done before; tell me, therefore, the way, for thou knowest, seeing that thou rangest the world like the sun himself, seeking the welfare of all."

So Narada, greatly pleased, had compassion on Dhruva, and said, "Thou mayest go even as directed by thy mother. Go to Madhuvana, where Hari is; bathe in sacred waters and sit on sacred grass; control all organs of sense, and think on Hari alone."

So Dhruva set out for Madhuvana, and Narada passed on his way and entered the city of King Uttanapada. Him the sage found pale and unhappy, and asked the cause. Thereupon the king confessed his cruelty to his little son; now, said he, the lad was sure to be devoured by wild beasts or die of hunger and weariness; an evil thing it was to be ruled by women. But Narada replied, "Be comforted; thou knowest not thy son's might. He will accomplish that which is difficult for even the greatest, and will in the end return, having greatly enhanced thy fame." So the king was comforted, meditating on his son's future greatness.

Meanwhile in Madhuvana, Dhruva day by day brought his senses under stricter control, and month by month increased the concentration of his thoughts. Under the stress of his doings all creation was vexed, and at length an embassy was sent to beseech Hari either to check the prince's austerities or to grant him the boon he sought. The god replied that the latter prayer would be granted, and, relating the story of Dhruva, bade them fear nothing. Then he mounted Garuda, and went forth to Madhuvana. There Dhruva, by concentration of spirit, had gained an inward vision of the divine form; and when Hari drew near, the prince's eyes were withdrawn from the sight of outward things. Then the god withdrew that inward image from Dhruva's thoughts, and at once the lad started from his trance and saw the god in visible form. He sought to utter praise, but, too young, he knew not how; whereon the god touched his cheeks, and Dhruva, filled with understanding, broke into hymns of praise, long and rapturous.

In the end the god, well pleased with this adoration, said, "I grant thee a place hard to reach and gained by none other; when thou hast in turn enjoyed the kingdom, thou shalt possess the region round which gods and Rishis ever circle. Weary of the world, thy sire will soon retire to the woods, and thou shalt reign 63,000 years in perfect health. After that shalt thou attain my region, to which all creation bows down."

So spake Vishnu, and Garuda bore him back to his heaven. As for Dhruva, he did not at once experience fullness of bliss; for he was set on wiping out reproach cast on him by Suruchi, and did not at once seek final salvation. Yet he could not but chide himself for this devotion to objects not the highest, feeling himself to be like a man of slender religious merit, who, going to an emperor, asks for broken grains of rice mixed with husks.

Thus he went to his father's city. King Uttanapada could scarce believe the joyful news, and went forth to meet his son in a golden car, surrounded by Brahmans, elders, friends, and kinsfolk, to the merry sound of horns, kettledrums, and pipes, the two queens following in a car. The monarch embraced his son with tears, and Suruchi, who had scorned him formerly, now raised him with blessings as he bowed before her. His father then bestowed on him special apartments in the palace, magnificently furnished, beset with lovely trees, shrubs, and tanks, where birds and bees disported themselves joyously. Then the king heard the tale of his son's prowess, and marvelled greatly. At length, satisfied with all he saw, and wearied with work, he retired to the forest.

Then it came to pass that Uttama, Súruchi's son went a-hunting one day, and was slain by a Yaksha on the mountains; and Dhruva, left in undivided possession of the kingdom, went forth to avenge his death. The Yakshas, resisting valiantly, poured on the king such clouds of arrows that he disappeared from sight, and the saints on high began to lament. Then, as his foes began to raise the shout of triumph, the chariot of Dhruva arose from the tumult, like the sun emerging from mist; and the king, stretching his awful bow, spread terror and havoc among his adversaries; and like the wind shredding the cloud-wrack, so he scattered the hostile ranks. As the levin cleaves to the innermost parts of a hill, so clave he the bodies of his foes through shield and harness; and the field was covered with broken mail and mangled corpses. To withstand this dire onslaught, the Yakshas, resorting to magic, caused terrific disturbances of nature and weird illusions, to baffle the king. But he laid a dread mystic weapon to his bow, and in a twinkling all the fabric of illusion was riven to shreds. Then once more he assailed them; they fell by thousands, and were in sore straits.

Hereon, seeing Dhruva destroy the Yakshas thus ruthlessly, Manu, father of the Human race, sought to stay him, and charged him with passion and malice in thus slaughtering thousands who were in no wise guilty of his brother's death. Kuvera, lord of the Yakshas, might well be wroth, and this resentful spirit ill fitted one who had attained to direct knowledge of Hari. So Dhruva desisted; and his foes rendered praise and homage, and Kuvera himself thanked the king for checking the fierceness of his anger.

Then Dhruva returned to his kingdom, praying that the knowledge and remembrance of Hari might never waver; and for thousands of years he ruled his subjects honourably. In the end, he turned once more to the pursuit of contemplation, and went forth on pilgrimage, gaining more and more an entrance to communion with the Supreme.

At last there descended for him a splendid chariot,

wherein sat two deities. These said to him, "Thou, who at the age of five years didst win the region of Vishnu, which the seven Rishis themselves contemplate but cannot attain, art now called to ascend this car and mount to that place—the region to which all the Universe bows down!"

So King Dhruva mounted the heavenly car amid the loud sounding of celestial music, and went up to the region of Vishnu beyond the three worlds, while heavenly beings on every side sang honour to the prevailing merit of Dhruva who had gone to the forest, a broken-hearted child of five years, and in a few short years attained that glorious state which others scarcely win after long practice of asceticism through many births.

Luminous spheres wheel round his high abode for ever; and there he shines, the great Pole Star, like the flawless crest-jewel of the three worlds.

Turn we now again to the Naga lord Aswatara and his two sons.

In answer to their sire's request, the princes related how their friend had told them the following history of his great adventure.

There came once to King Satrujit, the prince's father, a worthy Brahman, leading a noble steed, and said, "O king, a certain evil Daitya is grievously troubling me in my hermitage. Day and night he assumes the form of a lion, elephant, or other beast; and when I am engaged in some act of devotion, the foul fiend interrupts the same and robs me of the hard-earned fruit of my austerity. Thus vexed, one day, in the heaviness of my heart

The Meeting of Kuvalayaswa and Madalasa

I sighed deeply; and thereon fell from heaven this horse, and a voice was heard, saying, 'This steed can traverse unwearied the whole circuit of earth with the sun; he can course unstayed through sky and sea and the nether world. For thee has he been produced, and Kuvalaya is his name. Take him to King Satrujit; for his noble son, mounted thereon, shall slay the base Danava who vexes thee and shall win to himself a deathless name.' Obedient to the heavenly voice, I have brought the steed to thee, O King; give commandment therefore to thy son, as it was spoken, that thy righteousness may endure."

So King Satrujit took the horse, and, calling his son, mounted him thereon; and the prince, taking the name Kuvalayaswa,* departed with the sage on his honourable quest. Dwelling for a season at the Brahman's pleasant hermitage, he overcame every obstacle that stayed the performance of holy rites.

Then the vile demon, incensed against the sage and full of pride and arrogance, not knowing that Kuvalayaswa dwelt there, took on him the form of a hog, and drew near to do despite to the saint's evening sacrifice. Whereon, roused by the outcry, the prince leaped on his horse and pursued the boar; and drawing his mighty bow, smote it with a crescent-tipped shaft. The beast, sore wounded, fled apace through the great forests, but the magic steed followed hard upon him.

Thousands of leagues were thus covered by hunter and hunted. Then, on a sudden, the flying boar

* *i.e.*, 'whose horse is Kuvalaya.'

fell into a yawning chasm; and the king's son, ever close behind, fell likewise down the steep abyss through thick darkness. And when he saw things clearly again, lo, he was in Patala; but the boar had passed from sight. Then, faring on his way, the prince saw a great and glorious city, with lofty ramparts and hundreds of golden palaces. Entering this city, he wandered to and fro, seeing no man; but anon he saw a woman hastening along. Her he questioned, saying, "Whither goest thou?" But, answering not a word, she ascended into a palace: and he, wondering much, but wholly without fear, followed where she led.

There, in a room of the palace, he beheld, reclining on a golden couch, a solitary maiden, large-eyed and lovely in every limb. Then the king's son, gazing on her marvellous beauty, thought her none other than the goddess of the underworld. And she, beholding his noble features and stalwart frame, deemed him the god of Love himself. Surprised and abashed, the fair maiden stirred tremulously on her couch, asking within her mind whether this were indeed the god, or some Gandharva or Naga, or, again, some hero of surpassing worth. Seeing her confusion, the prince bade her fear nothing; and the other maiden, soothing her distress, took a fan and fanned her; so she revived—for indeed she had swooned.

When the maiden was fully assured of her safety, her companion told her story as follows: "This maiden, Madalasa by name, is daughter of the king of the Gandharvas. A fierce Danava, a dweller in Patala, found her in a garden, and brought her hither. However, it was foretold that, even though carried off, she would be rescued, ere the Danava could wed her, by one who should pierce the ravisher with arrows in the world of men. And I, O hero, am the lady's companion, Kundala by name; and, my husband having been slain, I go on pilgrimage from one place to another, preparing myself for another world. As to the Danava, he went forth to the upper world in the form of a hog, to vex certain sages at their sacrifices; and there, it seems, he has been smitten by some one, even as it was foretold. And as for this maiden's fainting, know of a surety that it was through love of thee; for at first sight she has become enamoured of thee, and none other will please her as a husband. Tell us, therefore, I pray thee, whom thou art! Art thou god or Gandharva, Naga or Daitya? For to this place mortals come not; and thou seemest of more than mortal make."

Then answered Kuvalayaswa, "Hear the whole matter shortly, honoured lady. I am the son of King Satrujit, and was sent by him to protect from demons the hermitage of certain pious sages. Then came one in the guise of a hog to thwart them; whom I, leaping on my steed, smote with a crescent-tipped shaft, and pursued as he fled. In the end, the enemy fell into a great chasm, and I after him. After wandering to and fro, I met thee, lady, and followed thee into this palace. As for my race, I am neither god nor Gandharva, but a mortal man, to whom gods are objects of worship, fair Kundala."

Then the heart of Madalasa was glad, and she

blushed with joy, gazing into the face of her friend. And Kundala said, "O hero, happy is this maiden at thy tidings; for clearly it is thou who hast fulfilled the prophecy concerning the death of the vile Danava. Therefore take her, O hero, happy in her lot, and perform the wedding ceremony according to rule."

So, there being no priest present, the prince himself took fuel and sacred grass, and kindled the holy fire; and, being learned in sacred lore, he recited the texts and caused the fair maiden to take part in the rite.

Then Kundala said to her friend, "Now that thou hast gotten a husband, fairest, my heart's desire is fulfilled, and I may go my way to perform all manner of penance and pilgrimage for the cleansing of my sins."

Shortly she spake yet again to the twain, saying, "To thee, O man of mighty intellect, even thine equals cannot offer counsel; how much less, then, a woman such as I! Yet, for love to this my sweet friend, I am bold to speak before thee, O conquering hero. Let thy wife be unto thee thy other half, by union with whom religion, wealth, and love come truly within thy grasp; without whom, these three things are scarce to be come at by any man. So, too, for woman there is neither religion, wealth, love, nor offspring apart from a husband. Take, therefore, each the other, to love and to cherish; and prosper together in riches, children, happiness, and length of days." So saying, she embraced her friend, and departed to do that of which she had spoken.

Immediately the son of Satrujit set his bride on the

Kuvalayaswa slays the Danavas

noble steed and made haste to depart with her. But the Danava folk saw it, and cried out that their pearl of maidens was being carried off together with the goodly weapons which the prince had won by his conquest of the fiend. So they called on him to stop, and assailed him amain with showers of arrows. But Kuvalayaswa, foiling their attack with a laugh, as though all were mere sport, seized a mystical weapon and hurled it at the Danavas; and thereby they, with the prince's special foe among them, were on the instant reduced to a heap of bones charred by furious heat.

Having thus vanquished his foes, Kuvalayaswa came with that pearl of women to the city of his father; to whom he forthwith related the manner of his finding her, together with the tale of his pursuit of the fiend and the conquest of the Danava warriors.

Hearing these things, Satrujit was filled with joy, and embracing his son affectionately, said, "Happy am I in thee, my son, who hast thus delivered the holy sages from their fears! The fame that I received from my ancestors I myself have increased; and now thou, in turn, hast added yet more thereto. He who neither increases nor lessens the fame transmitted to him is the ordinary man; he who launches forth into some new venture, whereby that fame is enlarged, is truly great. Thus I might, in my day, have delivered the Brahmans from the presence of the fiend; but thou, by thy descent to Patala, hast achieved a far more notable exploit; and henceforth thou art great among men, nor needest any whit to lean upon thy father's fame.

Therefore, my son, joy and success be thine, and may thy wife and thou ne'er be parted."

With these and other kindly words, the king again embraced his son, and suffered him to depart. So for a happy season Kuvalayaswa lived in his father's city, or in the country around, gladdened by the love of his fair bride; while she, too, lived in sweet harmony with his parents, by whom she was greatly beloved.

Then, in time, it came to pass that Satrujit again said to his son, "Go forth, my son, on thy noble steed, to patrol the earth, and rescue the saints in their hermitages from the assaults of the base Danavas who go about in hundreds to hamper holy men. So Kuvalayaswa went forth and patrolled the earth, as his father bade him, in defence of the saints.

Now among these Danavas was one Talaketu, brother to him whom the prince had overthrown. This wily fiend took the guise of a sage, and made him an hermitage on the banks of the River Yamuna. Then, when Kuvalayaswa passed by, the disguised Danava made petition to him, saying, "O prince, who art sent for our defence, I have a work to do, and I come to thee for aid. I must needs perform a holy rite to Varuna, Lord of the waters; give me, therefore, for gold thy neck-ornament, and guard my hermitage while I am absent."

So the prince undid the ornament that was upon his neck, and gave it to Talaketu with courteous obeisance, saying, "Go thy way, reverend sir, and do as thou sayest in peace of mind. None shall molest thy dwelling meanwhile, for I shall stay here, according to thy command, till the hour of thy return."

Then Talaketu plunged into the waters of the river, while the prince remained guarding the dwelling of the false hermit. But the base Danava made haste to go to the city of Satrujit, and there, in the presence of Madalasa and others, he told the king a lying tale, saying:

"The hero Kuvalayaswa fought, near my hermitage, with a certain vile Daitya, who went about to disturb the pious practice of holy men; and in that strife the Daitya, by use of magic, pierced the prince's breast with a spear. Ere he died, the prince gave me this neck ornament, and after his death his body was burned hard by. His noble steed, too, was led off in triumph by the wicked Danava. Now, therefore, O king, let all needful rites be duly performed without delay; and take this neck ornament for your comfort, for we ascetics have no dealing with gold."

So he spake, and departed. But all present, believing the lying report, were overwhelmed with grief, and both king and people lamented loud and long. And the hero's wife, Madalasa, hearing of her lord's death, endured not the pang, but quickly yielded up her life.

Whereupon great was the cry on every side, both in the houses of the citizens and also in the palace. The king himself, however, restrained his grief, and sought to console the people, saying, "It becomes us not—not even me myself—to bewail my son and his wife, who have undergone the stroke of fate. For, look you, if my son hath indeed given up his life in protecting the twice-born from the assault of fiends, he will assuredly rise to a higher existence. As for this lady, why should we bewail her, who has joined her husband in death? Wives have no true life apart from their husbands; and those are rather to be pitied who live on, separated from their lords. So lament not for my son and his wife, nor for us, his father and mother. For he who has given his life in defence of the righteous has brought weal to all alike, and has paid his debt to parents, Brahmans, and to duty; and my son, though he be dead, has yet kept unharmed the good fame of himself, his parents, and his ancestors."

To the same purpose, also, spake the queen, Kuvalayaswa's mother, saying, "No such joy came to my mother or my sister as has been mine in hearing that my son has given his life in battling for the defence of the holy sage. Those who perish in misery, wasted with illness, may well be accounted to have been born in vain. But those who, never turning their backs on suppliants, friends, or enemies, die in battle for a good cause, are indeed men and heroes, the pride of their mothers."

Meanwhile the Danava Talaketu, having returned to his country, came forth from the waters of Yamuna and spoke courteously to the prince, saying, "Go thy way now, O prince; for, thanks to thine aid, the business on which I was bent has been successfully performed."

Thereupon the king's son did him reverence and, mounting his noble charger, departed swift as the wind, for the city of his father. Arriving thereat, he beheld the city overcast with mourning, men going to and fro with sorrowful countenance; while the citizens, on lifting their eyes to the prince, were greatly amazed and brake forth into cries of joy, calling on him to hasten to his parents and relieve their sorrow. So he repaired to the palace, where his parents embraced him with more than common joy; and being moved with surprise, he questioned them and learned the whole truth. Then, hearing that the darling of his heart had ceased to live, he was plunged into a sea of shame and grief that she, so fair and virtuous, should have died for love of him. Mean, indeed, he felt himself to be, in comparison with a sacrifice so costly, and worthless seemed life without her. Yet, composing himself in his distraction, he meditated thus: "To what purpose shall I abandon life? How thereby should I benefit her who is dead? And shall I not thereby weaken those who are dependent on mine aid? As for lamentation, too, it beseems me not to weep overmuch; for I am a man, and should not come into contempt of mine adversaries. Howbeit, thus may I show my reverence for the memory of my beloved: I shall wed no other all my life long."

So he performed the funeral rites, and then made public his resolve that no other woman should ever hold the place of Madalasa whom he had loved and lost. And then, turning altogether from thoughts of woman's love, he gave himself once more to the companionship of other princes, and so continued.

Such was the tale of the Naga princes to Aswatara their father. But he took the close of the adventure amiss, and spoke of undertaking great austerities for the accomplishment of some high purpose; though what this purpose was, he told not to his sons. Forthwith he departed to the Himalaya mountains; and at the place where the sacred stream Saraswati rises, he practised great austerities for the favour of the goddess whose name the river bears. Long and fervently he chanted her praise, as the source of speech and song, rehearsing all the manifestations of her power, and imputing to her a sovereign influence in the highest concerns of the Universe. Then the goddess Saraswati, the mouthpiece of the gods, was favourable to Aswatara, and said, "I grant thee a boon, O Naga king; speak, therefore, and I will give thee the desire of thy heart."

"Grant me, then, O goddess," said Aswatara, "the mastery of every kind of sound!" So the gracious Saraswati answered him, saying—

"*Every sort of Verse and Rune,*
Every sort of Time,
Every sort of Tone and Tune,
Every Rhythm and Rhyme—
These I grant thee, all, and more,
Granted thus to none before."

Then that Naga lord, becoming possessed of this mastery of all that appertaineth to music, essayed with song to please the deity who dwells on the peaks of Himalaya, even the god Siva, and thereto exerted himself with all his skill morning, noon, and night. Thus praised, the god, blue-throated through drinking up the world-poison, was pleased, and granted the singer a boon. So Aswatara said, "If, O adorable three-eyed God of gods, thou art well pleased, grant that Madalasa, the wife of Kuvalayaswa, may become my own daughter, having the same age and bodily perfection as she did when death came on her."

Then answered Siva, "So be it, as thou desirest, most noble Snake-lord; and on this wise. When a certain offering is made, eat thou the middle portion thereof, and that fair lady shall forthwith rise from thy middle hood, in the form she bore when death came on her."

Without delay Aswatara went and did as the god commanded; and fair Madalasa was once more brought into being; but for the time the Naga king told no man, and kept the fair lady carefully hidden in the inner apartments.

Meanwhile the two Naga princes resorted, as before, to the company of their friend on earth, and disported themselves gaily as ever. But one day their father said to them, "Why heed ye not my words that I spake to you concerning your benefactor, that ye should do him some kindness in turn?"

So the twain, upon occasion, invited Kuvalayaswa to visit their home. But he replied, kindly, "Of a surety, this house is your home, and ye need go no farther to seek it; and if ye seek, of your kindness, to confer a benefit on me ye will best show me kindness by treating my home and wealth as your own; for my soul is knit to yours, and it pains me that ye should in any way think of yours and mine as separate." Then the Naga princes answered, "Be that according to thy will. Yet our noble father has often said, 'I would fain see that Kuvalayaswa!'" Thereupon answered Kuvalayaswa, "It shall be according to your father's wish."

So they went forth from the city and fared on their way. And in due course the two princes led the son of Satrujit into the goodly realm of Patala, and there they were changed into their proper form before him; and he marvelled greatly as he beheld their jewelled hoods and brave markings. Then they told him of their father, Aswatara, the Naga king; and he had great pleasure in all he saw in the fair underworld, observing the handsome dwellers therein, and being charmed by the sound of pipes and drums and tuneful song on every side.

So they went on and entered into the king's palace, where sat the lordly King Aswatara, clad in heavenly raiment dight with noble gems, on a golden throne overlaid with multitudes of jewels. Here the princes made Kuvalayaswa known to their father, who raised him up from doing obeisance, and embraced him lovingly, and said to him, "Long mayest thou live, and be victorious over all thy foes! The fame of thy virtues has reached me even before thy coming; long may they thus continue! The man who lacks virtue is dead while he liveth; but he who is virtuous brings good to all in heaven and earth, and all desire his welfare."

And to his sons the king said, "Let us now eat and drink and be merry to our heart's desire, and then shall we have further sweet converse with the son of Satrujit." So a great feast was prepared, and the king, with his sons and Kuvalayaswa, feasted royally, according to his word.

Afterwards the king, his sons being in attendance on him, said to the son of Satrujit, "Now, friend, declare what benefit I may confer on thee, our guest; behold, all the goodness of our house is before thee—doubt nothing, but ask even what thou wilt." Then said Kuvalayaswa, "Great king, in my father's house are gold and jewels in abundance; truly I have need of nought. Their lot is a heavenly one who possess, even in their father's lifetime, some small portion of his wealth, together with soundness of body and well-matched friends. Hard indeed is the lot of those who, early losing parents and wealth, have the burden of family cares without the proper means of support. Sufficiency of wealth delivers one from the need of making petitions to one's friends; having this, therefore, I would rather ask nothing."

Then the Naga king, smiling kindly, replied to the prince, the friend of his sons, "If thy mind be not set on gold or jewels, then ask something else; spare not to speak, whate'er it be!"

Then Kuvalayaswa answered again, "My lord, if I have deserved aught at thy hands, know that the debt has been fully paid in this, that I, a mortal, have embraced thy body, which is divine. Howbeit, if thou wouldst add to this thy kindness, then pray for me, that the pursuit of righteousness may ever be the first thought of my heart. That, in truth, is the root; good works, springing therefrom, are the tree; and wealth and objects of pleasure are the fruit, even the reward of good works in this life."

"So shall it be," said the Naga king. "Yet it remains for thee to choose some boon ere thou leavest this place. Gold and the like thou hast in the upper world; seek, then, something which thou deemest hard to obtain there."

Strange thoughts came to the mind of Kuvalayaswa, and he looked keenly at the faces of the young princes, his friends. They, in turn, fell down before their father, and, as though opening the matter to him for the first time, said, "Our noble friend had a lovely wife, daughter of the Gandharva king; and she, on hearing a vile Danava's false report of her husband's end, endured not to live, but quickly gave up her life. Then our friend made ever this vow, "None shall be my wife in place of my lost Madalasa." So now he earnestly desires to have a vision of her, if it may be contrived."

But Aswatara replied, "Such power belongeth only to those who are free from these gross elements. How may this be done, save as a dream, or by some trick of Sambara, master of magic?"

Then said the son of Satrujit, bowing low before the king, "If thou show me my Madalasa, even by illusion, I shall hold that thou hast bestowed on me a boon supreme."

"If thou ask it, my son," replied Aswatara, "I must perforce grant the request; for a guest's prayer is law. Therefore turn thine eyes hither."

Then the Naga king, muttering some gibberish in order to bewilder them, led in the fair Madalasa from the inner chambers of the palace, and showing her to the prince he asked, "Is this thy wife Madalasa or not?"

Then Kuvalayaswa, crying out "Beloved!", made towards her to embrace her. But Aswatara bade him stand, saying, "Beware, my son! 'tis but illusion; touch the same, and the vision vanishes immediately."

Instantly the prince fell swooning to the ground, and, half revived, thought woefully of his loss. "Ah me," he said to himself, "that this king, through kindness, should bring me thus to shame by reason of my sorrow for my wife. Illusion it doubtless was; though of what sort, I comprehend not."

Then King Aswatara raised him up, and told him the whole truth, how he had won Madalasa from the kingdom of death; and that it was she herself in true bodily form, for her husband to take to himself again. So there was great joy among all present; and thereafter Kuvalayaswa, taking his beloved, mounted the noble steed and departed to his father's home, where their wondrous home-coming gave cause for untold rejoicing and festivity. Happily did the prince and his wife live together; and when King Satrujit died, Kuvalayaswa succeeded him, and ruled his kingdom wisely.

Thus did the young hero, by his simple and unswerving devotion to his lost wife, gain for himself the unequalled esteem of his noble friends, and won, through their help, a reward past hope and above all price.

Chapter V

THE TALE OF SAVITRI AND SATYAVAN

[This Tale, and that of Nala, which follows it, were told by certain Rishis to the Pandava Brethren, of whom we shall hear in the last Tale of this book, to comfort them at times of great discouragement.]

THERE lived once a noble and virtuous monarch, ruler of the Madra folk, beloved of all; Aswapati was his name. He was devoted to the good of all, long-suffering, and truthful in everything; but, alas! he had no children. Therefore, being now stricken in age, and fearing that his line would die with him, he betook himself to devotions and keen penance, if thus he might come by offspring. For eighteen years, stinting himself in food and pleasures, he did sacrifice and honour to the divine Savitri; and when the eighteenth year was now fulfilled, the goddess became gracious to him. Rising in beauty from the midst of the fire-offering, she manifested herself to him with kindly mien; and thus, with bounteous intent, she addressed the king:

"Well pleased am I, O King, with thy self-control, penance, and hearty devotion. Choose thee a boon after thine own heart, O Madra monarch!"

Then answered Aswapati, "'Twas for the sake of offspring that I essayed this quest of merit: I would have sons, O goddess, to bear my name! If thou art pleased with my doings, this is the boon that I would choose; for the twice-born speak of offspring as a supreme necessity."

To him replied the goddess, "Of old I knew of this thy desire; and by the favour of the Blessed One there shall be born to thee a daughter of radiant fairness. This I tell thee, nor needest thou say more."

When the goddess passed from sight, the king returned to his home; and anon—for the promise spake of early fulfilment—there was born a fair-eyed girl, to whom, in honour of the goddess, the Brahmans gave the name of Savitri. The maiden grew up to early womanhood exceeding fair, even as the Queen of Beauty in bodily form; and folk gazing on her, slender-waisted and bright as a golden statue, thought in themselves, "A very daughter of the gods!"

Yet, for all her radiant loveliness, none asked her hand in marriage; for men were daunted by her very beauty. She, therefore, having duly fasted and bathed, and having done sacrifice, spake of this matter to the Brahmans at the auspicious season, and obtained their favour. Then she approached her father, and having bowed to his feet stood before him with folded hands. And he, beholding this daughter of his, now growing to womanhood,

K

beauteous as the immortals, was moved to sorrow by her pleading.

For it should be known that in ancient India—and not less so, indeed, to-day—it was esteemed a reproach to both father and daughter if a maid was not bestowed in wedlock at an age when we should count her but a girl.

"'Tis true, daughter," said the king, "the time for giving thee in marriage is come; yet none asks thee of me. Therefore choose thee thyself a husband, thy peer in virtue. To him whom thou choosest will I give thee, according to thine own desire. For thus it is written in sacred lore: 'A father who gives not his daughter in marriage, a husband who provides not, and a son who provides not for his mother when her husband is dead: these three are to be blamed.' Therefore bestir thee in quest of a husband; and so do, that I underlie not the reproach of the gods."

Having thus spoken, the king bade his daughter go forth to other lands in the company of aged counsellors. And she, bidding him farewell, mounted a golden car, with staunch retainers round her, and set forth through lovely woods, where royal sages dwelt as hermits. To these she made reverent obeisance, and everywhere gave rich gifts to Brahmans; and thus passed through forest after forest and country after country.

II

In those days the lord of the Madras was visited by the Rishi Narada. And while he, on a day, sat in the assembly in friendly converse, behold, Savitri drew near, having journeyed through all places of pilgrimage and was now returning home. Seeing her father thus seated with Narada, the maiden bowed her head to the feet of both in salutation; then said Narada:

"Whither went the maiden, and whence comes she now? And wherefore is she not given in marriage, in this her youthful bloom?"

Then answered Aswapati, "For that very purpose has she been sent on the journey from which she now returns. Learn from her own lips, O Rishi, whom she has chosen as an husband."

Thus bidden by her sire to tell the matter fully, the maiden spake thus: "There ruled over the Salwas a noble earth-lord, Dyumatsena by name. When blindness came upon him, his kingdom was reft from the heir, who was yet a child, by an enemy. Therefore Dyumatsena betook himself to the forest with his wife and son, and practised austerity with steadfast purpose. That son of his, born in the city and grown to manhood in the forest, Satyavan by name, is the husband of my choice."

"Alack!" quoth Narada, "truly Savitri has done amiss in this choice of Satyavan to be her lord." But these words he spake aside, it would seem, for the others heeded him not. Then again he spake, saying:

"Truth-teller is his sire, and truthful his mother; rightly, therefore, is the son called Satyavan—the Truthful."

Then Aswapati questioned Narada, saying, "Is this prince majestic and prudent, and patient as he is bold?"

"Majestic is he," replied Narada, "as the Sun in heaven, and the peer of Vrihaspati in counsel; bold as great Indra, and patient as Mother Earth."

Again the king asked, "Is this Satyavan generous and devout? Is he handsome, high-minded, and holy?"

Said Narada, "In generosity, piety, and truthfulness, he is even as the famous kings of yore; he is high-minded as Yayati, and kindly as Soma."

These and other words said Narada in praise of Satyavan. Then said the maiden's father, "As thou tellest his virtues, holy sage, so acquaint us with his faults, if such he has."

To this Narada made answer, saying, "He has but one fault, against so many virtues; but this fault is one that cannot be lightly set aside. In one year from now his life-span runs out and he must quit this body."

Then said the king, "Hie thee hence again, Savitri, and choose another husband! A great fault this, despite many virtues, that, as the holy Narada hath said, a single year must bear away his allotted span of life."

But his daughter answered, "Once only falls the lot, once is a maid bestowed in marriage, and once for all is a gift given; these three things are done once for all. Let him be long-lived or short-lived, virtuous or worthless, him have I chosen as husband once for all, and none other will I choose. Thus have I determined in my mind, and thus have I spoken with my voice; let the proof come in action, for this is my resolve."

Then said Narada to the king, "The maid is steadfast in her purpose, and cannot be turned therefrom. And, in sooth, such virtues are in Satyavan as in no other man, and the bestowal of thy daughter thus pleases me well."

"So be it," said the king, "as thou sayest, I will do even thus, for thou art my teacher."

Then said Narada, "Let there be no hindrance in this wedding of thy daughter. Fare ye all well!" And having thus said, he ascended from the earth and passed to high heaven. And the king made speed to set forward the preparation for the wedding.

When all her raiment was brought together, he summoned the aged Brahman priests, and set forth with his daughter on an auspicious day. To the forest they went, and made lowly salutation to royal Dyumatsena in his hermitage, where they found him seated on the grass, bereft of sight.

Having thus made obeisance, King Aswapati prepared to present his petition, not without an offering of suitable gifts. Having received these, Dyumatsena asked the king the purpose of his coming, and the other made known to him the matter concerning his daughter and Satyavan, praying that Dyumatsena would receive the maiden as his daughter-in-law.

Then answered the blind king, "We, fallen from our high estate, do practise penance and austerities in this forest haunt. How shall thy daughter, all undeserving of such a portion, endure this hardness?"

"Nay," quoth Aswapati, "seeing that my daughter understandeth well both the joys of prosperity and the sorrows of adversity, this word of thine troubles me not. I pray thee, of thy kindness, combat not my hope; for thou and I are well fitted to be acquainted, the one with the other. Take, then, my daughter to be the wife of the noble Satyavan!"

Then said Dyumatsena, "In truth, O king, I have long desired some bond with thee; but with the falling from my kingdom, I put the thought from me. Now my old desire returns amain, and thou art a welcome guest."

Then the two kings, having summoned all the Brahmans who dwelt around the hermitage, caused the wedding to be celebrated in due form; and Aswapati, having thus bestowed his daughter, and fitting raiment with her, returned home with a joyful heart. Satyavan, likewise, gaining a wife endowed with every virtue, rejoiced exceedingly; as did she, receiving the husband of her wishes.

When her father was gone, Savitri laid aside all her ornaments, and donned raiment of bark-cloth; and by service of every sort, by her labours and humility, she won the hearts of all, and especially of her husband's parents. Him, too, she greatly pleased by her kindly speech, deftness and peaceable demeanour, and by many quiet ways of service.

Thus passed the days in that forest dwelling, happily enough, to all appearance. But Savitri's heart was heavy, and oft she stood day and night thinking of the word spoken by Narada. Nearer and nearer came the day when Satyavan must die, and Savitri thought ceaselessly thereon, reckoning the time with care. And when she reckoned that but four days remained, she set herself to stand unmoved for three days and nights. Hearing of which heavy task, the king was troubled, and rose and spake thus to Savitri, soothing her anxiety:

"Too sharp is the trial which thou essayest, princess; hard indeed it is to stand thus for three nights."

But Savitri answered, "Fret thee not, good father; I shall win through this vow right well—it wants but perseverance."

Then answered Dyumatsena, "Far be it from me to bid thee break thy vow! 'Win through!' is even what I myself would say." Thus spake Dyumatsena, and refrained; and Savitri abode there, standing immovable. Heavy was her heart indeed, as the last night passed, bringing the day that was to see her husband die.

Then as the day dawned, she made offering to the kindled fire, and, when the sun was risen a space, performed the morning's duties. Thereafter she saluted all the holy Brahmans and her husband's parents, standing before them humbly with folded hands. And they all, in kindly mood, heartily commended her prayer, earnestly desiring that she should never know widowhood. For to this end did wives in those days perform such vows; though it would seem that neither the Brahmans nor the king himself understood clearly the doom that lay on Satyavan. But Savitri, expecting ever the dreaded moment, brooded on Narada's words with stricken heart. Then said the king to his wife, kindly:

"The vow set before thee has been worthily performed. Now is the time for food; do thou partake forthwith."

But Savitri replied, "When the sun sets, then shall I eat with an easy mind; such is the desire of my heart, and the time appointed by me."

Then, even as she thus spake concerning the taking of food, came Satyavan himself, with axe on shoulder, prepared to go into the wood. But Savitri cried to him, saying, "Go not alone to the wood! I would fain go too, for I cannot bear to leave thee."

"Nay, dear lady," said Satyavan, "thou hast ne'er gone to the wood hitherto; the ways are rough; and how canst thou go afoot, thus spent with fasting?"

Then answered his wife, "From fasting I have neither faintness nor weariness; stay me not, thus bent on going with thee."

"If go thou must," said Satyavan, "I will even do thy pleasure; but seek leave of my parents first, lest blame light on me."

Then Savitri went to them, and, after salutation, said, "Yonder goes my husband to the wood in quest of fruits. Fain would I go with him, if ye, O parents, suffer me so to do; for I can scarce bear to leave him now. If ye hinder him not, then hinder not me, I pray you, but suffer us both to go together. For nigh a year have I ne'er been forth from the hermitage, and I am right eager to see the flowery wood."

Then said King Dyumatsena, "Since the day that Savitri came from her father's hand, I recall no request from her lips; let this her prayer, then, be granted. Only see, daughter, that thou trifle not by the way."

Thus, her petition granted, that noble young wife went forth in her husband's company, with smiling face, yet with heart full sore. Wide-eyed she gazed

"Savitri Laid down her Husband's Head" 152

on the delightful woods around her, all gay with peacocks and the like; and beheld goodly streams, and princely mountains all a-flower. Sweet was her husband's voice, calling her to look on this or that. But as she watched his every movement, she remembered the sage's word, and thought each moment her lord's last. Thus she followed him, treading softly, her heart tossed this way and that, as she awaited the fatal hour.

III

Then these two gathered the needful fruits, and filled therewith a vessel. Thereon Satyavan addressed himself to hew wood, so that the sweat brake forth on his body; and with his toil, his head began to ache. So he turned, aweary, and spake thus to his wife:

"Dear Savitri, the labour has brought pain to my head; my limbs and heart ache, as it were, and I feel my whole body ill at ease, for 'tis even as though sharp points pierced through my head. I would fain sleep a space, sweetheart, for in truth I scarce have strength to stand."

So Savitri made her husband to lie down; and sitting beside him, she took his head in her lap. In that moment, as she thought of the Rishi's prophecy, she was aware of a man in red raiment, tall and majestic, but red-eyed, with noose in hand, and awful in presence, who stood by the side of Satyavan and gazed upon him. Beholding him, Savitri laid down her husband's head and arose; and with folded hands, all trembling, she thus addressed the stranger:

"Truly I know thee for a god, for thy presence is more than man's. I pray thee, great deity, say whom thou art, and what thy purpose is."

Then answered the stranger and said, "A good wife art thou, Savitri, and hast borne much for thy husband's sake; therefore I speak thee fair. Know, fair lady, that I am Yama; and, as to my purpose, the sand of thy husband's life has run out, and I would bind him and bear him hence."

Then said Savitri, "Surely it hath been told me, blessed one, that thy messengers are they who bear men hence; how, then, art thou come thyself for my husband, O lord?"

Thus questioned, the lord of Shades, to do her kindness, did thus expound his purpose: "This husband of thine is dutiful, handsome, a very ocean of virtues; 'twere not fitting that my attendants should bear him, and therefore am I come myself."

Thereupon Yama drew forth from the body of Satyavan the soul, of the size of a thumb, and bound it fast; and the body, reft of vital breath, fell back, limp and lifeless, a sorry sight to see. Then Yama, having bound the soul, set forth toward the south; and Savitri, sore at heart, but strong-souled and steadfast in her vow, followed after him. But Yama said to her, "Turn, Savitri, and perform the funeral rites! Thy debt to thy husband is paid, and thou hast come as far as thou mayest."

Then answered Savitri, "Whither my husband goes, thither am I also bound to go. To this my penance, loyalty, and affection entitle me, and thy favour should permit my going. The wise, who know the truth of all things, say that friendship may be established by going seven paces with another; on this friendship, therefore, I would fain speak a word. In the forest, men without self-control do not observe the ordinary rites of civilised life. But by domestic regularity one may compound all other rites, and having this one needs neither a second nor a third duty. So the wise consider domestic faithfulness the chief of all things."

Then said Yama, "I am well pleased with this word of thine; choose thee, therefore, what boon thou wilt, saving only the life of Satyavan."

To him Savitri thus replied: "Fallen from his kingdom, my husband's father dwells in the forest, bereft of sight. By thy favour let the king regain his sight and be restored to strength and majesty."

Then answered Yama, "This boon I grant thee according to thine own words, O blameless one, and even thus shall it come to pass. But in this journey I see naught but faintness for thee; so hie thee back, and let not weariness o'ertake thee."

But Savitri replied, "How should weariness o'ertake me near my husband's side? For there my place must ever be. Where thou leadest him, thither my steps are bent; so hearken to another saying. 'A single meeting with the good is greatly to be desired; and friendship with them is to be prized above all.' Fellowship with a good man can ne'er be fruitless; therefore one should abide in the company of the good."

Seldom, doubtless, was the lord of the dead thus flattered by the praise and the company of living mortals; so he answered again:

"Very pleasant to me is thy prudent speech. For

this, choose thee another boon, saving, always, the life of thy husband."

Then answered Savitri, "Grant that the king, my father-in-law, may regain the kingdom that was taken from him, and that he may ne'er again thus lose his rights."

And Yama answered, "He shall regain his kingdom, and that right soon; nor shall he fall therefrom again. Now that thy desire is granted, turn again.

But Savitri answered again, "Thou art he that restrains men, and therefore is thy name called Yama*; hear me yet again. Mildness toward all beings, in deed and word and thought, favour, and generosity—these are the duty of the righteous. And they show mercy even to their enemies."

This hint at further favour was not lost on Yama, who replied, "As drink to the thirsty, so is thy speech to me. Ask, therefore, another boon, saving only thy husband's life."

Then said Savitri, "My father has no children save me; grant him a hundred sons, that his name may continue in the earth."

And Yama answered, "A lusty stock of a hundred sons shall he have, to maintain his family among men. And now, turn thee homeward, princess, for already thou hast come far."

But Savitri refrained not from following the lord of the dead, and plied him with further soft speeches. After each word, Yama would grant her some other boon, ever excepting the life of him whom he had come to take away. But as the drop wears out the stone, not by force, but by often falling, so the

* From the Sanskrit root *yam*, "to restrain."

faithful wife at last won her way with the stern god, and he said:

"Again am I well pleased with thy words; choose, therefore, loyal wife, through my great regard for thee, a boon unrivalled!"

Then cried Savitri, "Let no exception be made in this, as in the other boons! For this boon, I choose the life of Satyavan! Without him, I am even as dead; bereft of him, I long for neither pleasure, daylight, nor life itself. In one boon thou didst grant to me a hundred sons"—for such had been one of Yama's promises—"how, then, could'st thou take my husband from me? Let Satyavan live! Thus shall thy word be found faithful."

Thus she spake; and the lord of justice with right good cheer loosed the bonds of Satyavan, and thus addressed Savitri:

"Behold thy husband loosed by me, noble lady, and restored to soundness! Thou mayest take him hence, and happy shall he be; for four hundred years with thee shall be his portion of life, and he shall win good fame among all men. An hundred sons ye twain shall have, kings and warriors all; and such, likewise, shall your parents have, brothers to thyself, like unto the immortals."

Then the glorious king of justice, having granted her heart's desire, gat him to his own place again; and Savitri turned to the place where lay her lord's body, uncomely and lifeless. Sitting on the ground, she raised him, taking his head in her lap; and anon consciousness came to him, and he spake thus to Savitri, his wife, looking up at her long and lovingly:

"Deep has been my sleep—wherefore was I not awaked? And where is yon grim stranger who drew me to him?"

Then answered Savitri, "Deeply hast thou slept on my breast, O hero. The stranger was the god Yama, from his realm; and he is gone. Now thou art rested, my lord, and the sleep is gone from thee. Arise, if thou canst; for see, the night is descended."

Then Satyavan, having fully come to himself, like one awaking from sweet sleep, cast his eyes around him, and spake thus:

"We went forth, we twain, in quest of fruits; and anon, with hewing wood, I took sore pain in the head; by reason of which, being scarce able to stand, I laid me down and slept, my head upon thy lap. Thus far I remember, but thereafter sleep stole my senses, as I lay fondled by thee. Yet, hold! I saw then a stranger of great stature and grim aspect. Tell me of him, fair one, if thou knowest; did I behold him in dream or in truth?"

But Savitri answered, "See, the night descends—to-morrow I shall tell the whole matter. But now rise up and seek sight of thy parents; the night has come down and the sun is gone. Night-roving creatures, of fierce presence, bestir themselves amain, and sounds of movement are heard throughout the forest; and hearing their cries, I am seized with trembling."

"Fearful, truly," said Satyavan, "is the wood, thus wrapt in darkness. Scarce wilt thou discern the path; how then can we go homeward?"

Then said Savitri, "In the wood there stood a dry

tree a-burning, the flame whereof, fanned by the wind, may yet be seen somewhat. By feeding that flame with these logs, I shall make light. But if thou art yet unable to walk—for the pain may still be with thee—and canst not discern the path in the shadowy wood, let us bide here this one night, till the day dawns."

But Satyavan replied, "The pain is gone, and I feel my limbs sound once more, and I would fain have sight of my father and mother. Never have I been so long absent from the hermitage, for my mother ever expects me before fall of even. Doubtless they look eagerly for my coming, so long delayed. I, too, would know their state, and deep will be my grief if I find them not. Ere now they have besought me tearfully—that aged pair, so dear to me—saying, "Without thee, dear son, we live not for an instant; only while thou remainest is our life firm within us. In our old age and blindness, thou art our staff and the support of our line; on thee we lean for funeral offering and fame and future offspring! My mother will surely be troubled for me, as I for her; and my father is blind and helpless. Surely I live for them, and they should be upheld and kindly treated by me."

Thus speaking, Satyavan, devoted to his aged parents, flung up his arms and wept aloud. But Savitri, seeing her husband thus distressed, wiped away his tears and comforted him. Then Satyavan spake again, saying:

"I would fain have sight of my parents, Savitri, and that soon. If evil hath come on them, I shall not endure life. Therefore, if thou wouldest have me live, I pray of thy kindness, let us go together to the hermitage."

Thereon Savitri arose, and dressed her hair, and aided her husband to stand upon his feet. And he, having thus arisen, and having laved his limbs in water, gazed around, and his eye lighted on the vessel with the fruit. But Savitri said, "To-morrow mayest thou bring in the fruit; meanwhile, I shall bear the axe myself."

Therewith, she drew her husband's arm over her left shoulder, and putting her own arm round him stepped forth on the way. Then said Satyavan, "The path I know from experience, and I perceive it also by the moonlight that falls betwixt the trees. Yonder the path divides in twain; take the turn to the north, and go with speed, for I am sound and strong again, and yearn for the sight of my parents."

IV

About this hour, King Dyumatsena on a sudden received his sight again, and lifted up his eyes round about. And seeing his son nowhere, he went with his wife from one hermitage to another, seeking him. On they hastened, distraught, with feet wounded and blood-stained, and bodies torn with grasses and thorns. Then the Brahmans from other hermitages took them back to their own resort, and comforted them with kindly words and tales of ancient kings. But as they thought of the boy's doings in his early days, their grief broke forth afresh, and they called pitifully on their son.

Then said one of the Brahmans, "As surely as

Savitri is devout, humble, and attentive, so surely Satyavan lives."

Another said, "I have studied the Vedas and all that appertains to them, and have laid up great store of merit, and have practised all manner of vows and fasting. By virtue of these austerities I know certainly, and would have you assured, that Satyavan lives."

The Rishis also came, and added their words to these. "Savitri," said they, "is endowed with every auspicious mark, showing that she will never know widowhood; Satyavan, therefore, lives yet."

They spake severally, also, of Savitri's high and wife-like virtues, and of Satyavan's princely gifts; to the end that the parents might believe that their son was yet alive and would live long.

Now, as the king and his wife began to take comfort from these many words, behold, Savitri drew near with Satyavan, and entered the hermitage with great joy. Thereat, the Brahmans, seeing their words fulfilled, hailed the king with wishes of long prosperity, assuring him, too, that it would come ere long. They also kindled a fire and did homage to Dyumatsena, and all sat down happily together. Then these forest-dwellers, moved by curiosity, inquired of the prince, saying:

"Wherefore comest thou thus late at night, lord, and not betimes? What hath befallen thee? Thy father and mother have been sore troubled, and we would fain hear all."

Then answered Satyavan, "With their permission, Savitri and I went forth; and pain in the head came on me as I clave wood. Through this pain, I fell asleep and slept long; ne'er before have I slept so long in this wise. Be not therefore troubled; for this alone is the cause of our late return."

Then said one of the sages, "We would know, too, how thy father Dyumatsena came by his eyesight. If thou knowest not the cause, haply Savitri can tell. Thou, Savitri, art like the divine Savitri in radiance, and doubtless knowest the reason of this thing. Speak, therefore, plainly, if thou art not bound to secrecy."

To him answered Savitri, "No secrecy is laid upon me; therefore hear the matter plainly. My husband's death was foretold by Narada, and this was the day appointed; therefore I would not leave his side. As he slept, Yama drew near in person, and, having bound his soul, sought to bear it away to the land of shades. Then I praised the god with many a true word, and he granted me five boons in turn; the first and second, that my lord's father should regain his eyesight and his kingdom; in like manner, a hundred sons for him, and a hundred for mine own self; and lastly, that my husband should not die, but live four hundred years, seeing it was to this end I underwent my vow. This is the whole matter plainly told—a tale of much grief, though the end thereof is joy."

Then said the Rishis, "Thou, sainted lady, by the goodness and sufferings has delivered this family, overwhelmed by evils and sinking in the lake of darkness." And having thus praised that pearl of women, they bade farewell to the king and his family, and departed with light hearts to their own place.

V

So the night passed, and the sun's orb rose again. Then the sages came once more together, after the morning sacrifice; nor could King Dyumatsena hear often enough the tale of Savitri's achievement.

And it came to pass at this time, that messengers from the Salwas came to the king, telling how that enemy of his was slain by the prime minister; and how, after it was known that the usurper, with his friends and kin, was slain, the hearts of the people were as the heart of one man toward their old king. "Be he blind or not," said they, "he shall rule over us, and he alone."

"With this purpose," said the messengers, "have we been sent—even to bring thee forthwith, O King. Set forth, therefore—for the city rings with blessings on thy name—and sit on the throne of thine ancestors."

So Dyumatsena, with wife and family, set forth in a car drawn by men, surrounded by his army. Great was the wonder and joy of the folk, beholding their king no longer blind. The priest anointed him to be king once more with right good will, and anointed Satyavan as heir to the throne. In due time were born the hundred sons promised to the king, likewise those of Savitri and Satyavan.

Thus did Savitri by her faithfulness deliver from ruin her husband and her parents, his family and her own; and great was her fame among all men. And even so, said the sage who told the tale, would the Pandava brethren be rescued from affliction and despair by the woman they loved.

Chapter VI

THE TALE OF NALA AND DAMAYANTI

THERE ruled of old over the Nishadas, said the sage, a prince named Nala, ennobled by every kingly virtue and learned in holy writ, but having this fault—too common among Hindu warriors—that he loved the dice too well.

In those days also lived another monarch, Bhima, King of Vidarbha, a prince of great might. For a long time he was childless; but in the end there were born to him certain valiant sons, and a fair daughter, the pearl of maidens, whom he called Damayanti.

The excellencies of Nala and Damayanti became so widely known, that each often heard the other's surpassing worth loudly praised; and so it came to pass that each meditated much on the other's noble virtues, and meditation grew to love, though they had never met.

Then, one day, King Nala, walking in his palace grounds, saw the swans with gilded wings sporting through the grove, and caught one of the fair birds. But the swan besought him to spare its life, saying,

"If thou spare me, I will fly to Vidarbha and sing thy praises to the fair Damayanti."

So Nala gave the bird its life, and away it flew with its companions, and in Vidarbha extolled the merits of Nala in the presence of Damayanti so cunningly, that the princess readily gave the bird an answering message of love to bear home to Nala.

Therewith, both these young people became sad and pensive with the growing burden of mutual love. And King Bhima, seeing his daughter thus, took thought that the time was come to seek her a husband. So tidings were borne to divers kings that Bhima's fair daughter would hold her Swayamvara,* that he whom she should choose would be her husband.

So many a noble earth-lord, with princely train of elephants, steeds, and chariots, drew near to Bhima's court; and among them came King Nala. But it chanced that the gods, too, had knowledge of the Swayamvara, and it pleased the celestials that they, too, should compete for the maiden's love. So they descended from the skies in their heavenly cars, and, seeing Nala faring eagerly on his quest, called on him to be the bearer of their message to Damayanti, to choose one of them as lord, whether it were Indra, the Thunder-god, or Agni, the lord of Fire, or Varuna, whose sway is over all Waters, or Yama, ruler of the Shades.

Sore troubled was Nala by the gods' behest, and sought to be excused; but the gods would not be

* Literally, Own-choice' of a husband by a high-born maiden. See the "Tale of the Pandaav, Brethren."

denied. By their might, therefore, Nala was swiftly transported to Damayanti's bower, and stood before the maiden, while she and all her company stood amazed both at the manner of his coming and at the matchless beauty of his person. King and princess gazed with deepening love on each other, and the maiden was as loth to hearken to Nala's message as he to give it. In the end, she bade him bear word to the immortals to be present at the great gathering of all the kings, to abide her choice, with intent that there, where her word was law, she would name Nala as her lord before gods and kings.

But when, in the hour of her Swayamvara, she came forth to speak the word of choice, behold, the four gods had all donned the guise of Nala himself, and she saw five of his form and garb, all undistinguished one from another. Then she adjured the gods piteously to reveal themselves; and they, in kindness, showed the signs of their divinity even in their disguise. Then joyfully Damayanti named the true Nala as her chosen one, and loud was the acclamation of the people and the lament of the rejected princes.

Then the gods bestowed on Nala, as wedding gifts, eight great powers: Indra granted him a godlike gait and power to discern the deity in every sacrifice; Agni gave him power to call forth fire at will, and sway over worlds of light; the lord of Death gave him subtle taste in food, and supreme constancy in pure virtue; while from Varuna he had power to summon water at will, and unfailing supply of fresh garlands. Then the bridal was splendidly celebrated; and anon Nala bore his lovely bride back to his Nishad realm,

"The Maiden was loth to hearken to Nala's Message" 166

where he ruled justly, in supreme happiness, many days.

But it chanced that a deity less kind—in fact, a very spirit of evil—learned of the Swayamvara too late, and resolved, in his bitterness of spirit, to ruin King Nala, who had won the fair prize. Long this evil one watched and waited for a chance to catch the king in some slip from his duty; but twelve years passed in vain. However, as all things come to those who wait, the opportunity came at length, and the evil spirit entered into Nala and possessed him. Then, at the spirit's call, Pushkara, Nala's brother, drew near, and challenged the king to play dice. This challenge Nala might not refuse; but he wist not that the evil one had also bewitched the dice, to work his bane. So these twain played, and not once nor twice, but ever and again, King Nala lost. Citizens and counsellors sought to turn him from the play, but he received their words as one that hears not; messenger after messenger did the gentle Damayanti send, but all to no purpose. On and on went the baleful sport, till the distraught king had lost not only his wealth, but even the kingdom itself.

Then said Pushkara, with evil smile, "Throw me one more hazard, brother, for Damayanti herself—she is all thou hast left to stake!" At that word, King Nala rose speechless, and slowly left the place; and taking his wife, wandered forth from the scene of all his royal happiness, banned by his cruel brother, in desperate straits even for food and drink.

Thus, scantily clad, they strayed woefully into the

forests, and Nala counselled his wife to leave him and seek the protection of her kindred. She, however, in a voice half-choked with grief, said that she would never leave him so; but if indeed it were well for them to seek Vidarbha, let them go together, and her noble father would gladly receive and succour him. To this the proud soul of Nala would not stoop; so they turned again to their wandering, and came to a rude hut in the wood, where king and queen laid themselves down on the cold, hard ground to rest. Damayanti slept, overcome with weariness; but Nala could not rest for agony of mind. Then, as he gazed on her sleeping, the evil spirit moved him to think of deserting her. "If I cleave to her," thought Nala, "she will ever have sorrow and hardship; parted from me, she may yet come by relief. As for danger in her loneliness, her virtue will be her shield."

Reasoning thus with perverted mind, King Nala basely left his wife as she slept. And she, waking later, shrieked aloud in dismay and terror, yet scarce would believe, at first that he was really gone, calling fondly to him as though he had hid himself for a space only to try her courage and love. Then, crying aloud his name, conjuring him to return, reproaching his faithlessness, lamenting the distraction which had driven him to so wild a deed, and his loneliness when parted from her, she hastened onward wildly, plunging deeper and deeper into the savage wood. Of a sudden, a monstrous serpent seized her, helpless, but was slain by a hunter of the forest; then her rescuer, in turn, tried to woo her from loyalty to her husband, but fell, slain by her

"They gazed on her with Wonder" 168

indignant curse, like a lightning-blasted tree. On she strayed through densest forest; past streams, pools, and lakes; past hills and through valleys; seeing every sort of beast and bird, and monsters neither beast nor man.

After much wandering, she came to the forest abode of some pious hermits; and these received her kindly, and foretold to her a happy issue out of all her trials. But when they had thus comforted her, behold, they and all their dwellings vanished utterly; and Damayanti, sore amazed, took up her uncertain travel once more.

Next she fell in with a goodly caravan of merchants, and they gazed on her with wonder; for though thin and travel-stained, she was still of surpassing beauty, and some thought her a nymph or sylvan goddess, while others desired to hear her story. So, in a few words, she told them the tale of her woes; and the merchants received her to their protection, saying that they were bound for the realm of Subahu, king of Chedi. So the caravan set out again, and stayed for the night on a fair lawn, by the margin of a lovely lake studded with lotus-flowers.

Then, in the depth of the night, when all slept, came a herd of wild elephants to drink at the lake; and these, scenting the tame elephants of the caravan, were suddenly inflamed with rage. Fiercely the ponderous brutes charged, and helpless to resist were all that stood in their way. Some were slain and some escaped by flight; woe and lament resounded on every side, both of those stricken and of others bewailing the loss of their goods. These, wildly questioning each his neighbour for what sin or lack of divine service they had been smitten, cried out on a sudden that the wild maiden, whom they had found, must needs be a witch or fiend, and they sought for her to slay her forthwith. But she, hearing in good time their angry talk, fled to the depths of the forest, lamenting the misery which she seemed to bring on others, and also the hopelessness of her own lot.

Then, in company with certain Brahmans who had escaped the slaughter, she made her way to the city of Subahu, king of Chedi. And here too, as she entered, men observed her with wonder; for they remarked her noble bearing and uncommon beauty showing through the marks of sorrow, hunger, and wandering, even as lightning breaks through murky clouds. As she thus passed through the curious crowd, the king's mother spied her from the palace, and bade her old nurse go forth and bring her in. "For surely," said she, "despite her worn and wild looks, yon maid is fair as heaven's queen herself."

So the nurse went forth, and brought the hapless Damayanti before the queen-mother, to whom she told, in part, her sorrowful tale. And the queen-mother welcomed her, and bade her live in peace and safety with her, while the king's messengers were sent far and wide to seek tidings of Nala. So Damayanti was comforted for the time, and dwelt in the palace with the queen's young daughter, Sunanda by name, to tend her wants.

* * * * * *

Meanwhile King Nala wandered on sadly, remorse gnawing his heart. Ere long, he saw in the forest a mighty fire, out of which a voice called to him for help. Nala hastened to the rescue; and lo, it was the King of the Serpents that called, and Nala paused when he saw this. But the Serpent bade him be without fear, and said, "Know that I lie here through the curse of the Rishi Narada, whom once I angered; and he bade me lie thus till one Nala should pass by. Free me therefore, O King, and I shall do thee noble service in return." Therewith the Serpent shrank to the size of a thumb, and Nala took him up lightly and bore him out of the fire. Then suddenly, as he moved slowly onward, the Serpent bit him, and straightway his kingly form was all changed and marred. While he marvelled at this, the Serpent said, "For thy good have I done this, O King! By this poison the evil spirit in thee shall suffer grievous torment, and thus, in the end, thou shalt be delivered from him. Also in this guise thou shalt not be known, which, for the present, is to thy profit. Further, the poison now in thee has the virtue of making thee proof against all pain. Now get thee to Rituparna, King of Ayodhya, and engage thyself to him as charioteer under the name of Vahuka; teach him thy skill in training steeds, and he in return shall teach thee his mastery of dicing. When thou wouldest regain thy true form, don these garments which I give thee; and rest assured that thou wilt yet regain wife, kingdom, and happiness." So saying, the Serpent-king gave him two magic vests, and vanished from his sight. Then Nala went to Ayodhya, as the serpent had bidden him, and Rituparna willingly engaged him as charioteer. Yet sadly did he pass his days, sighing oft for the wife whom he had so cruelly left.

In those days King Bhima, in his anxiety, sent forth Brahmans to go and seek Nala and Damayanti in every city. Of these Brahmans one named Sudeva came anon to the city of Chedi; and there, in the palace, he saw fair Damayanti, still marred by exposure and want. So he obtained access, and courteously made known his mission to her, and she wept freely when she thus talked with the good Sudeva. Then Sunanda, seeing her weep, told it to the queen-mother, who came where the twain stood together and asked Sudeva to declare his knowledge. Thereto Sudeva replied, "Lady, this is the daughter of King Bhima, the wife of King Nala, who has lost his all in dicing and now roams the earth, parted from his wife, we know not where. To seek them we Brahmans have been sent by King Bhima, and on this quest came I hither; here I spied this lady, and, drawing nearer, knew her by a birth-mark to be Damayanti without doubt."

On this the queen-mother, shedding tears of joy, turned to Damayanti and said, "Thou art mine own sister's daughter—all that I command here is thine!" Then Damayanti, joyfully accepting her kinswoman's greeting, said, "Loving, indeed, has been all my treatment here; yet it were well, methinks, if thou permit, that I should now go with those who have sought me out. Suffer me, therefore, to go to my home and my little ones."

To this request the queen-mother gave consent, and Damayanti returned to the home of her father Bhima. Gladly they welcomed her there; but her first concern was to gain tidings of her husband, and at her request King Bhima sent forth Brahman envoys, whom Damayanti charged that, wherever they went, they should, as if addressing Nala himself, say in the hearing of every gathering of men some such words as these, "Whither wentest thou, O gamester, leaving thy devoted wife, meanly clad in half a garment, in the dreadful forest? Hear my prayer, and return to me, as thou art in duty bound." Then should these Brahmans take note if any present were caught by the words or moved to answer.

So they departed to do her bidding. And after many days one of them returned and told Damayanti that, when he had spoken her message in the court of Rituparna, a charioteer named Vahuka, all deformed in body, had been much moved by the tale of Damayanti's desertion, and had marvelled greatly at her willingness to forgive all.

Then Damayanti sent secret word to the Brahman Sudeva to go quickly to Ayodhya, Rituparna's city, and to publish tidings that she, Damayanti, was once again about to hold a Swayamvara. She also promised Sudeva a bounteous guerdon if he should contrive Nala's return.

When these tidings came to Rituparna's ear, he bade the seeming Vahuka make ready the chariot, for he would fain seek to win Damayanti himself. Sore rent by grief was the heart of the disguised Nala, for he wist not whether this was the act of Damayanti's despair or her stratagem to draw him to her presence. Howbeit, he gave ear to the command and chose, with a shrewd eye, four goodly chargers to bear the chariot on its long journey. Then the king mounted the car, and Nala, with an assistant charioteer, set the steeds to the road.

Scarce had they started when, under the magic touch of Nala's matchless guidance, the steeds sprang aloft in the air and sped like wind o'er river, forest, and hill. Greatly marvelled King Rituparna; and the thought that the misshapen Vahuka might be none other than King Nala in disguise—so great was the fame of Nala's driving—crossed his mind. But Rituparna had gifts of his own, no less wondrous than Nala's skill with horses. Pleased to show his wit, in rivalry with that of Nala, he counted, even as they flew past, the leaves and fruit on the branch of a tree; and when Nala, at the king's command, tore away the branch in passing, lo, the number, though running to myriads, was found to be exactly as the king had said.

The king then spoke of his skill in dice being fully as great. On the instant, Nala offered to impart to him his own knowledge of horses in return for like instruction in the science of dice. No sooner had Nala received this knowledge than the evil spirit that possessed him came forth, and Nala, though racked with dreadful throes, became once more his own master.

Now the journey drew to an end; and Damayanti, hearing the thunder of the rattling car, thrilled with joy, feeling sure that Nala himself was nigh. King Bhima knew not of Damayanti's wily message concerning the Swayamvara, and marvelled somewhat at the coming of his royal friend; and Rituparna, not knowing of Bhima's ignorance, answered cautiously when questioned as to the cause of his visit. Yet the two monarchs were glad to meet, and Rituparna was courteously entertained. But dismay fell on

Damayanti's spirit when she saw with Rituparna none but the seeming Vahuka and his assistant. So she sent one of her maids to question this Vahuka, whether he knew anything of Nala and his wanderings. Then Nala, with much emotion, told how a Brahman had come to his master's court, and how he bore a strange message concerning one who had left his wife in the forest. Then the maid returned and told what she had heard to Damayanti, and she, believing that the deformed charioteer was indeed her husband, bade the maid go back and watch the man carefully. So the girl went, and came back with a strange tale. The charioteer, she said, was wondrously gifted beyond all other mortals; when he approached the lowly doorway, the lintel raised itself to give him passage; at his wish came forth abundant food, and water for every vessel; he had but held a bunch of grass towards the sun, and straightway fire was kindled, and this fire he handled freely without scathe; and lastly, at his touch withered flowers revived to greater beauty and fragrance than before.

Then Damayanti bade the maid go once more and take by stealth some of the food which Vahuka was preparing; for Damayanti had often tasted the food prepared by the magic skill of her husband. And when brought, no sooner had she tasted it than all doubt vanished, and in great emotion she cried out that Nala and Vahuka were assuredly the same.

Yet once again she sent the maid, bearing the two young children, to Vahuka's presence. And he, moved to tears, folded them to his bosom; yet even so he revealed himself not, but spake of their resemblance to his own two children, and courteously advised the maid to come no more.

Now could Damayanti contain herself no longer, but broke her hopes and fears to her mother, entreating that he whom she thought to be her husband should be brought to her presence, and the matter put to the test and decided forthwith.

Greatly moved were both when they stood once more face to face; and Damayanti, addressing her husband still as Vahuka, said mournfully, "Heardest thou ever, Vahuka, of one who, for all his fair repute, left his wife asleep and undefended in a lonely wood? Yet even so did Nala, the noble king, leave me, his true and loving wife, the mother of his children!"

Then Nala, beholding her weeping pitifully all the while she spake, answered sorrowfully, "The guilt was not mine, but the evil spirit possessed me and drove me headlong into that fury of gambling and despair. The wretch has now been cast out of me after suffering long days of misery through thy curse and my religious penance; so the end of our sorrows is now in full view. Yet say thyself, noble lady, how comes it that thou, leaving the memory of thy plighted husband, hast sent forth word of choosing another lord? For it was even on this report that King Rituparna has hied hither in such haste."

Then Damayanti, trembling at the charge thus levelled in turn at herself, answered saying, "No guilty intent was mine, 'twas but a wile to draw thee hither! The Brahmans sent forth by my father to seek thee brought word that at Rituparna's court was one resembling thee in all but outward shape;

and I schemed hereby to draw thee hither forthwith. May all the powers that witness the ways of mortals testify against me and condemn me, if I have swerved one whit from loyalty of heart to thee, for whom I rejected both gods and men!"

Then the Wind, the watcher of all things, spake from the air, "Nought hath she done, O King, in despite of loyalty to thyself all these three years that ye have been parted, and this matter of bringing Rituparna hither was but a shrewd device to bring thee thyself. Fear not, therefore, but take thy loving wife to thyself again."

Then sounded heavenly music, and flowers fell from on high, and, on the instant, the strange disguise passed from Nala and he stood before Damayanti in his proper form; they embraced as those may who have been parted so woefully, and pledged their love anew over their sweet babes.

Strange indeed to Rituparna was the unveiling of the truth concerning his misshapen charioteer and her to whose supposed Swayamvara he had made so swift a journey. Howbeit, he greeted the restored Nala most courteously, and each acknowledged his debt to the other. Then Nala imparted to his late master his wondrous skill in the management of steeds, as Rituparna explained to Nala his mastery of dicing; and therewith Ayodhya's monarch returned to his own city.

Then, after certain days, Nala set forth with a goodly following to his ancient realm, and called on Pushkara, his usurping brother, to meet him once again in a contest with the dice. "All," said he, "I hazard on this one meeting; and, if thou shrink from this form of rivalry, then put we the matter to the test of arms!"

Pushkara had no thought of perilling himself in armed fight with his warlike brother; but of his own skill in dicing he stood in no doubt, and in his vain confidence he talked loudly and lightly of this new victory, which was to bring him not only a further assurance of the kingship and all that appertained thereto, but the lovely Damayanti also, on whom his heart still doted.

Grimly controlling his fury, Nala bade his brother cease from idle talk and address himself to the contest. And then, lo, at a single throw, all that was lost came back to its rightful owner—monarchy, treasure, and all. Yet, in his triumph Nala fell not from nobleness of mind towards his fallen brother. Sternly, indeed, he condemned his vanity and folly; but vengeance, such as Pushkara's own conduct towards himself might well have been held to merit, he disdained wholly. He bade his brother go in peace, promising him not only life and safety but also a proper abode and portion of goods.

So Pushkara, after rendering to his brother the obeisance due to such royal clemency, abode for a space at the capital, having honourable entertainment, and then departed with a fair following to the city appointed for his portion.

This matter honourably settled, Nala returned to Bhima's royal city, to bring his Damayanti home. And Bhima, seeing her husband thus securely restored to his true estate, bade them farewell with tranquil mind, and sped them on their way with fatherly blessings and wealth of royal gifts.

If thus, said the sage who told the tale of Nala, it came to pass that beings even more luckless than the Pandavas won through their woes to a happy issue, then might the five brethren and Draupadi endure for a space, seeing, moreover, that a glorious future had been surely foretold for them if they would but stand fast for a season.

Chapter VII

THE TALE OF THE PANDAVA BRETHREN

IN olden days there reigned at Hastinapura, in northern India, a king named Santanu, the son of Kuru.

Santanu had two wives, named Ganga and Satyavati. The latter had already a son, named Vyasa, who became a great sage, learned in all things. After marrying Santanu, Satyavati had two other sons, both of whom died childless. Santanu's other wife, Ganga, had one son, Bhishma by name, who became a great warrior and a sage counsellor; but he, too, had no children.

The younger of Satyavati's later sons had married two wives; and after his death Vyasa married these widows, that the line of Santanu might not die out. One of them had a son named Dhritarashtra, who was born blind. The other also had a son, who was called Pandu, and he became king at Hastinapura when Santanu's sons died.

Like others already mentioned, Pandu married two wives, one of whom had already a son named Karna, whose father was the Sun-god; but the mother did not like this to be known, so her son Karna was brought up by a charioteer and his wife. Karna's mother then had three more sons, named Yudhishthira, Arjuna, and Bhima. The other wife gave two sons to Pandu, twins, named Nakula and Sahadeva. But these five boys were, in sooth, the sons of various gods. Yudhishthira was the son of Dharma, the god of Duty or Righteousness; Arjuna, of Indra, the Thunder-god; Bhima, of Vayu, the Wind-god; and the last two, of the Aswins, twin gods resembling the Castor and Pollux of the Greeks. These five brothers came to be known as the Pandavas, after the name of their father Pandu.

During the absence of Pandu, on occasions of war or hunting, his half-brother Dhritarashtra acted as regent. This Dhritarashtra had married a princess named Gandhari, and they had a hundred sons and one daughter. The eldest of these sons was Duryodhana, of evil name, who was ever the bitter foe of his cousins the Pandavas.

When Pandu died, his sons were taken to the blind king Dhritarashtra, who treated them kindly, and brought them up with his own children. But the Pandavas excelled their kinsmen in strength and manly sports, and great was the jealousy between the two families, especially between Bhima and Duryodhana, who were both of prodigious strength and violent temper.

As has been mentioned, Kuru was the father of Santanu, and therefore the ancestor of both Pandu and Dhritarashtra; both these families, accordingly, might be correctly called after him. But, in order to distinguish the sons of Dhritarashtra from the Pandavas, Duryodhana and his brothers kept the older family name to themselves, and were thus known as Kurus, or Kauravas, by which name we shall often speak of them.

It must be owned that some of young Bhima's doings were not such as to make him beloved of the Kaurava youths, when the two families played together; for he turned his great strength to many a sad prank. Sometimes he would seize his cousins by the hair and drag them along the ground: or, when some had climbed into a tree to gather fruit, he would come and shake the tree so furiously that the lads lost their hold and fell; or, again, at times of bathing in the river, he would hold them under water and only loose them when half-drowned. These rough jests filled the heart of Duryodhana with much bitterness, and he devised against Bhima a murderous plot.

He caused a fair pleasure-ground to be prepared on the banks of the Ganges, with every convenience for sport and bathing and banqueting. Thither he proposed that both families should go together, and the invitation was readily accepted by all. Sport of every kind was carried on with all good feeling, and at the banquet following Kauravas and Pandavas vied in showing each other honour and kindness. Duryodhana went to and fro among his rivals with a smiling countenance, and ministered dainties to Bhima himself with great show of brotherly love. But with these dainties baneful poison was mixed; and, as the day drew on, Bhima found himself oppressed with a strange weariness, and sank to sleep in the cool of the breeze. Then came his wily adversary, and binding him hand and foot as he lay insensible, cast him headlong into the Ganges.

Down sank Bhima, deeper and deeper, till he came to Patala, where the Nagas dwell. The snake-gods bit him in a thousand places; but, wondrous to relate, their vehement poison did but annul the venom of Duryodhana's drugs, and Bhima, instead of being consumed, regained consciousness. Daunted by this strange happening, some of the Nagas bare word to Vasuki, their king; but he was in no wise displeased, and made Bhima right welcome in the under-world. To restore the hero's strength, he ordered that jars of a magic drink should be set before Bhima, who through drinking eight of these became endowed with elephantine strength. Then the king gave him for the night a bedchamber of royal magnificence, and in due time restored him to the world of men, no worse, but rather the gainer by the perilous adventure.

The Pandavas, in the meantime, had returned from the pleasure-rounds without Bhima, supposing him to have gone before them. Great, then, was the commotion and distress when he was nowhere to be found, and grave suspicion fell on Duryodhana, whose cruelty and hardness of heart were so well known that such suspicion never did him injustice. But when Bhima reappeared, the Pandavas, for all their joy and triumph, chose to publish nothing of the matter, and constrained their mother likewise to hold her peace.

This was not Duryodhana's last attempt to poison

Bhima, nor did the other Kauravas—to their shame be it said—abstain from treacherous devices to compass the death of the Pandavas.

To mend these evils, Dhritarashtra appointed one Drona, the son of a great Rishi, as tutor to his own sons and the Pandavas together. Under his instruction both parties attained to great excellence in all warlike exercises. Arjuna was foremost of all in the use of weapons generally, but Bhima, Karna, and Duryodhana, also, possessed extraordinary strength and skill. Unhappily, this study of warlike arts under one master served but to fan the flame of rivalry betwixt the two families, as shall be shown forthwith.

When all the youths had been thus wholly instructed in the duty of warriors, they went forth together to fight against Drupada, king of the Panchalas, on account of an insult he had offered to Drona. He was duly conquered, but Drona kindly allowed him to retain half his kingdom. This Drupada afterwards became the father of a son named Dhrishtadyumna, and a daughter, Draupadi, of whom this tale has much to say.

The conquest of Drupada was due rather to the Pandavas than to the Kauravas; and on the return of the armies, Dhritarashtra appointed Yudhishthira heir-apparent. These doings greatly increased the jealousy of Duryodhana, and in his bitterness of spirit he devised a horrible plot to destroy the five brethren.

He caused a palace to be hastily erected in a wood, and courteously invited the Pandavas to occupy it. But this palace was built of everything combustible, and the base-hearted Duryodhana meditated in his heart to come one night and set fire to the palace, and thus destroy the Pandavas while they slept.

The brethren, however, received timely warning of the treachery, and escaped the snare. They went, indeed, to the palace, and dwelt there for a time. But while they abode there, they had a subterranean passage dug from the midst of the house. Then, on the appointed night, they themselves set fire to the palace, and escaped in safety by their passage.

Now, though the Pandavas knew it not, there had come to the house that evening a low-born woman with five sons; and these, having partaken of the good cheer too freely, fell into drunken slumber, so that they were consumed in the flames.

In the morning, the townsfolk came forth to view the ruin; and, finding the ashes of the woman and her sons, supposed them to be the remains of the Pandava family. Dhritarashtra was told that they had perished in the fire, and their funeral rites were performed amid general lamentation.

Meanwhile the Pandavas, having made good their escape, took up their abode, after sundry adventures, in the town of Ekachakra, where they dwelt for a space, doing good to the people, and being greatly beloved by them.

II

While the Pandavas thus lived at Ekachakra, they were visited by the Rishi Narada, who told them, among other things, more of the history of

King Drupada, and of the birth of Dhrishtadyumna and Draupadi.

This maiden, who had been in her last birth the daughter of a Rishi, was condemned at that time, owing to actions in a life still further back, to miss the privilege of obtaining a husband. She sought, therefore, to propitiate the god Siva, that she might win from him the choice of a boon. The deity, satisfied with her attentions, did even as she had hoped; on which she exclaimed, not once but often, "Give me a husband!" To this the god replied that her wish was granted; but, for the number of times that she had uttered it, she must needs have five husbands, whom she should win from the race of Bharat.

It was signified to the Pandavas that this prophecy would find its fulfilment in them, and they were counselled to go to the capital of the Panchalas and there await the turn of events.

Now the time was at hand when Draupadi should choose for herself a husband. For in ancient India it was the custom—far otherwise than it is in these days—that a maiden of high degree might invite suitors of equal rank to assemble on a given day in her presence, and might take a husband from among them by her own choice; wherefore the ceremony was called Swayamvara, that is, "Own-choice."

The news of Draupadi's Swayamvara having been bruited abroad, a goodly company of kings and princes assembled on the appointed day. Now Draupadi's choice was to be determined by no ordinary judgment of brave looks or rich attire and attendance, but by a contest of skill, for which a magnificent amphitheatre was prepared. All around were lofty palaces, having windows latticed with network of gold and walls bright with mosaics of jewels. All present wore fragrant garlands, and the air was laden with exquisite odours.

To this noble preparation came the Pandavas, in the guise of Brahmans; for as such they had come to the city, and lived as mendicants in the house of a potter. After two weeks of festivity and public enjoyment, the noble prince Dhrishtadyumna led his sister before the assembly, and in a voice far-reaching as thunder proclaimed the terms of the contest.

There, in the midst was erected a pole, on the top of which was set a golden fish, and below the fish a wheel spun round unceasingly. For the competing princes was brought forth a mighty bow, and five shafts thereto. He who could both string the bow and wing a shaft through the turning wheel to the eye of the fish should be Draupadi's chosen lord.

So the suitors essayed the task, but one after another failed even to string the great bow, till Karna, the half-brother of the Pandavas, came forward. Lightly he strung the bow, for great was his strength; but Draupadi, remembering the tale that went abroad concerning his birth, exclaimed, "I choose no charioteer for my husband," and Karna, who stood with the bow drawn to the full, laid it down sullenly and withdrew.

Then came Jarasandha, the great king of Magadha, noted for his strength, to try the bow; but springing backward, it felled him to the ground, so that the trial bade fair to prove too hard for all.

Then came the disguised Arjuna. In a twinkling he strung the bow and then sped the five arrows through the whirling wheel, straight to the mark. Loud rang the amphitheatre with the plaudits of the multitude, and the gods rained flowers from on high.

The assembled princes, however, were filled with fury; for, though the Brahman caste is highest of all, yet it seemed foul reproach to these Kshatriyas that they should be vanquished at their own sport by one who seemed to belong to a caste that has little to do with martial employ. So when Drupada seemed fain to bestow the maiden on him who—whate'er his caste—had won the contest outright, these kings gathered in wrath and prepared to assault their host. Arjuna and Bhima hastened to defend Drupada, and, after a vehement contest, the fear of Arjuna's mystic weapons caused the assailants to desist; whereupon it was proclaimed that Draupadi had been fairly won by the seeming Brahman, and was his by right.

Forthwith Draupadi departed with Arjuna and the Pandavas to the potter's house, where they were staying. They told their mother in jest that they were bringing what they had gained by begging; to which she, not seeing Draupadi, replied, "Share it among yourselves." Greatly was she dismayed when she found what her saying would mean; but the word could not be recalled—Draupadi must needs be the wife of all five brothers. And this, as we have seen, was but the fulfilment of destiny.

King Drupada, meanwhile, was still ignorant of the rank of him who had won his daughter at the Swayamvara—for he doubtless thought little of the

Brahman guise in which the Pandavas had appeared —and he therefore sent his son Dhrishtadyumna to see what he could learn of their rank and bearing. Listening outside the potter's house, the prince heard the brothers talk much of arms and war; and, pondering over the skill of Arjuna, together with what he had heard, he concluded that these were none other than the Pandava brethren, and thus he reported to his father. Drupada rejoiced greatly at the news, and sent noble chariots to fetch the brothers, that the wedding might be celebrated with becoming pomp. He doubted at first concerning the fitness of Draupadi's marriage with all five brethren; but Yudhishthira explained to him the prophecy about Draupadi, and the monarch debated the matter no longer. Draupadi was led round the sacred fire by each of the five brethren in turn, and thus became the wedded wife of all alike. Drupada crowned the nuptials with princely gifts, and like munificence was shown by the god Krishna, who was then on earth in human form and was present at the ceremony.

When Dhritarashtra heard that the Pandavas yet lived, and had won Draupadi, he took counsel how he should act towards them. Duryodhana and Karna were hostile; but the wiser counsellors bade the king deal kindly with the Pandavas, and he agreed to bestow on them a portion of his kingdom on the banks of the river Yamuna. Here the Pandavas erected a noble city, worthy to be compared with that of Indra himself; wherefore it was even called Indraprastha, which name is borne by part of the city of Delhi to this day.

Now, for all the happiness of this occasion, there was but too much chance of ill-feeling arising among the Pandavas concerning Draupadi, to whom all five were equally wedded. That such sad results might not mar their triumph in winning her, the Rishi Narada paid them a visit, and, to bring home to them the dire peril of strife betwixt brethren, told them

The Tale of Sunda and Upasunda.

These were the sons of a famous Daitya king, and were heroes of great might and fierce temper. They were—as became those whose very names had been formed each, as it were, to echo the other—united by the closest of brotherly love. Neither attempted anything of import apart from the other; together they ate and drank, together they played, together did they all that was worth doing. Each sought to please the other by word and deed; they were of one heart and mind, and were even as two persons made one.

So they grew up in great strength and valour, and their ambition was to conquer the three worlds. To this end they set themselves to do grim penance amid the Vindhya mountains. They were clad in raiment of bark, besmeared with filth, wasted with hunger and thirst, feeding on air alone. They offered their own flesh in sacrifice, and stood on tip-toe, with arms upstretched and eyes unwinking, for great length of time; so that, scorched by the fury of their austerities, the Vindhya mountains gave forth smoke, a wondrous sight to see. The spectacle of these penitential works moved the gods to great fear, and they sought to stay the brethren by various wiles. First they tempted them with various objects of pleasure; but Sunda and Upasunda heeded not, nor stayed their work of mortification. Then the gods devised illusions, whereby the brethren were made to see their nearest and dearest assailed by a furious fiend and crying piteously for help. But still Sunda and Upasunda heeded not, and the whole fabric of illusion passed away.

At last came the Father of gods and men, and offered the brethren even that which they sought—the choice of a boon. So they prayed that they might become perfect in the knowledge of magic and arms, strong and beautiful, and, lastly, immortal.

To this Brahma replied that all was granted, save immortality alone.

Then the brethren prayed that at least they should have no fear of death from anyone or anything in all three worlds, save from each other only. And this did Brahma grant: even that neither should fear death at all save by the other's hand.

Then Sunda and Upasunda, having gained their object, returned to their own place, and great joy came upon the Daitya folk as they arrived in triumph. They cast off their penitential attire, and donned spotless raiment and costly jewels. Eating and drinking, entertaining and merrymaking, singing and all manner of sport was the rule in every house, and the Daitya city rang amain with the riotous din of untrammelled revelry.

Having taken their fill of rejoicing after their

first success, the two brothers started forth to make proof of the powers conferred by Brahma's boon. They departed from the city with great pomp and with a mighty following, and fared forth to conquer the Three Worlds.

First they ascended to Indra's heaven with baneful intent; and at their approach the gods, knowing the boon granted to the brothers, departed in haste to Brahma's heaven. So the twain subdued the heaven of Indra, using all the denizens there right cruelly. Then they turned their might against the Nagas in the Underworld, and subdued them, and also all the dwellers in the seas. Then they gave their mind to earth once more, and spake fiercely to their followers, saying, "By divers offerings and sacrifices of sages do the gods maintain their strength. Turn we, then, with all our hearts, to the slaughter of all such foes of our race."

With these words, and this dark intent, they fell on the pious sages who tended the sacrifices of the gods; and wheresoe'er they found such, they wrought wholesale slaughter and destruction, and all the curses launched at them by the holy men scathed them not a whit, for the boon made them proof against all. The Rishis fled in terror from their hermitages, like snakes before Garuda, but the brethren pursued and slew them without stint or pity. Ceased were sacrifice and offering, slain were kings and Brahmans, woe and lament were on every side. Ceased were buying and selling, ceased the tilling of the fields and the tending of cattle; ruined were the cities, and the earth all unsightly, strewn with bones and skulls. Gloom o'ercast sun, moon, and stars, as they beheld the doings of Sunda and Upasunda.

So, having conquered every region, the Daitya brethren took up their abode in Kurukshetra, both being as yet unmarried.

Then gods, sages, and other exalted ones, with sun, moon, and stars, drew near to Brahma and made petition that he would devise some means to stay the deadly works of Sunda and Upasunda. The Father of gods and men meditated for but a moment, then summoned Viswakarma, the divine architect.

"Lend all thy skill," said Brahma to him, "to fashioning a maiden whose beauty shall have no rival in all Three Worlds."

So Viswakarma gave all his cunning to the task, and presently brought forth a maiden of such peerless loveliness, that the eyes and hearts of all that beheld her were utterly ravished. This damsel, to whom was given the name Tilottama, made obeisance to Brahma, and begged to learn what was required of her. "Go thou," said Brahma, "present thyself to the sight of Sunda and Upasunda, and be to them a source of jealousy and hatred!"

Meanwhile, the Daitya brethren were giving themselves up to the enjoyment of the triumphs they had won. Having taken the treasures of gods, Gandharvas, Yakshas, Nagas, and others, they revelled in these with supreme contentment. There was now none that could stay their enjoyment; and they abandoned themselves wholly to the fruition of all that could delight every bodily sense. In the goodliest woodlands and parks of the Vindhya mountains they roamed or stayed at will, surrounded by all that was fairest in nature and all by which art could minister to their pleasure. As they thus disported themselves to the utmost limit of enjoyment, Tilottama made her way towards this lovely region, plucking, as she passed through the forest, the flowers that grew on river banks.

Then the two brothers, elated at the moment by recent drafts of exhilarating drink, beheld the maiden on a sudden, and were confounded by the vision of her loveliness. Up sprang in each heart the seeds of love and rivalry. Each seized Tilottama by one hand; each glared suspicion and jealousy at the other; each claimed, in tones loud and fierce, priority in the right to the maiden's love. Such rivalry, in natures so proud and violent, could not keep itself within the bounds of speech and reasoning. Hands were raised, and deadly blows were struck; and down fell these two lordly Daityas in their gore, like two suns fallen from heaven, each stricken to death by a brother's hand.

Thus were these twain, whose might and steadfastness had raised them so high that neither god nor other celestial being, nor anything in the earth or under it, had power to scathe them or limit them in any way, utterly undone in a twinkling by a simple love quarrel between themselves.

So moved were the Pandavas by the solemn warning of Narada's tale, that they entered into a solemn covenant among themselves that, to prevent any root of jealousy springing up among them, whosoever should intrude upon the presence of one of his brothers when sitting with Draupadi, should be bound forthwith to spend twelve years of absence in the forest.

No long time went by, when Arjuna himself fell under the ban of this rule. It was, indeed, through no fault on his part; rather, it was through his kindness of heart; for, in order to succour certain Brahmans whose goods were being carried off by robbers, he had to go into the room where he knew Yudhishthira to be seated with Draupadi, in order to get his arms. Knowing the chivalrous purpose which had led Arjuna into the breach of their agreement, the brethren besought him to hold himself free from the ban; but the knightly spirit of Arjuna would not yield to their kindly persuasion, and he set forth from Indraprastha for twelve years of travel and adventure.

Among other places, he visited the city of Dwaraka, the home of Krishna, where the god, in his human nature, ruled over a great people, the Yadavas, who were, indeed, Krishna's sons. The family in which Krishna was born was descended from the same ancestor as was Kuru himself, so that Krishna ever showed himself greatly interested in both Kauravas and Pandavas.

On the occasion of this visit, Arjuna married Subhadra, Krishna's sister, bearing her off, victorious, from others who contended for her hand. When he returned from his exile, Draupadi was at first disposed to be jealous of the newcomer; but Subhadra humbly said to her, "I am thy slave," and Draupadi was appeased.

Not long after, the Khandava forest near Indraprastha was consumed by Agni, the god of Fire, much against the will of Indra, the god of Thunder and Rain. As Arjuna aided Agni in the struggle, this god gave him, as a reward, the great bow Gandiva and two inexhaustible quivers of arrows.

The Pandavas now dwelt in great happiness in a glorious palace, built for them by a Daitya, or Titan, named Maya, whom they had aided to escape from the burning Khandava forest.

Here Yudhishthira proposed, after a time, to celebrate the so-called Rajasuya sacrifice, in token of his power; but he was told by Krishna that he must needs first overcome and slay Jarasandha, the king of Magadha. A great conflict ensued, in which Jarasandha engaged in a hand-to-hand fight with Bhima, and was finally slain by him. The brothers then extended their conquests towards all four points of the compass, and on their return the Rajasuya sacrifice was performed with great pomp.

Duryodhana, however, who had attended the ceremony, returned to Hastinapura full of jealousy and hatred. In this frame of mind, he was advised by his uncle Sakuni to challenge Yudhishthira to a gambling match. No Kshatriya could refuse such a challenge; and Yudhishthira was fond of dicing, though he lacked skill, while Sakuni was an expert dicer and versed in unfair practices as well.

Accordingly the Pandavas were invited to Hastinapura, and Yudhishthira was challenged by Sakuni to play. In reply, he dwelt on the folly of gambling; but he could not refuse the challenge, and the fateful game began. Yudhishthira, no match for his skilful and unscrupulous opponent, lost throw after throw. Money, jewels, chariots, servants, and troops were

Draupadi dragged from her Chamber

staked in turn, only to be lost. Yudhishthira then ventured his capital, and all his public wealth; lastly, to the scandal of many of the onlookers, he staked Draupadi herself, and she too was lost.

Great was the joy of the Kurus. Duryodhana sent for Draupadi, saying that she should be a slave and sweep the chambers. She was dragged in by her hair by Duh-sasana, Duryodhana's brother, and grossly insulted by Duryodhana himself; and Bhima swore that one day he would drink Duh-sasana's blood and smash Duryodhana's thigh.

The Pandavas were now really slaves of the Kurus, but Dhritarashtra, out of compassion for Draupadi, allowed them to go free. Duryodhana and others, however, fearing that the Pandavas would return to recover what they had lost, sent them another challenge to play with dice, on the condition that the losers should retire to the forests for twelve years, and spend a thirteenth in disguise.

Yudhishthira played again, and lost as before, and the Pandavas were called on to depart to the forests. They laid aside their royal robes, and set forth in great humiliation; but amidst all, they showed that they cherished a good hope of return, and there were not wanting those who prophesied that, at the end of the thirteen years, they would come back and overthrow their foes.

III

After the brothers, with Draupadi, had lived some time in their forest, Arjuna, by Vyasa's advice, set forth in quest of special weapons by which he might the more easily conquer the Kauravas. To test his valour, the god Siva encountered him in bodily form, and after a tremendous conflict, in which Arjuna bore himself right well, presented him with a weapon of extraordinary power, as a reward for his bravery.

Arjuna passed through many adventures, and spent a considerable time in Indra's heaven, Swarga. The other Pandavas mourned his absence, and deplored the sadness of their lot. In their depression, they were comforted by various Rishis, who came and related to them sundry tales, showing the happy recovery of other mortals quite as unfortunate as the Pandavas, and imparted good counsel in various forms.

As the Pandavas went abroad in search of adventure, they were assailed by a fiend named Jatasura, who carried them all off, excepting Bhima, who was absent searching for golden lotus-flowers on a lake sacred to Kuvera, the god of Wealth. Bhima, however, came to the rescue of his brethren in good time, and slew the fiend. Not long after, he approached the abode of Kuvera, which was surrounded with great wealth of gems. The god's attendants went forth to repel him, but he vanquished them and slew many. On hearing of the slaughter of his myrmidons, Kuvera at first was very wroth, but anon he changed his mood, and said that Bhima had only done a warrior's duty.

In process of time, Arjuna rejoined his brothers, having been five years in Indra's heaven. He arrived in the car of Matali, Indra's charioteer, and gladdened his brothers with the account of his wondrous doings; among which the chief, perchance, was his fighting, at Indra's behest, against the Danavas—giants or Titans—whose millions he overcame by his heavenly weapons and knowledge of magic. Yudhishthira was fain to see Arjuna display these mystic weapons; but so dire was the effect on both earth and sky, that gods and sages at once drew near and advised Arjuna not to use the weapons without due reason.

Meanwhile Duryodhana and his friends rejoiced greatly on hearing news of the low estate of the Pandavas. Duryodhana even gathered a great force that he might safely go and gloat over their misfortunes. On approaching the forest, he was forbidden to enter by Gandharvas, the choristers of Indra's heaven. But Duryodhana defied them, and gave battle with his army. He was utterly overthrown and was taken prisoner by the Gandharva king; but, on the intercession of Arjuna himself, who was the king's friend, he was allowed to go free.

It is not necessary to recount all that befel the brethren during their years of forest life. Therefore only two more of these adventures shall be told ere the story of their return to public life is related.

It chanced that one day, when the brothers were a-hunting, Jayadratha, the mighty king of Sindhu, as he passed through the forest spied Draupadi, and, being filled with admiration, entered into conversation with her. He asked her to leave her present husbands and become his wife; and when she scornfully refused, he bore her away in his car. But the Pandavas, hearing the cries of birds and beasts, returned in haste, and at once pursued. Jayadratha was overtaken and defeated, and well-nigh slain by Bhima, who threw him down, and kicked and beat him. His life, however, was spared on his saying, "I am the slave of the Pandavas," and in the end he was allowed to depart in liberty.

The second of these adventures was a strange and dreadful one, which came nigh to causing the utter ruin of the Pandavas. It happened on this wise. Yudhishthira had gone with his brethren to the Dwaita forest, where dwelt a hermit. This man asked the Pandavas to recover his firewood, which had been carried off by a stag. This stag the brethren then pursued, but in vain, for it outran them completely, and in the end disappeared. The brothers then sat, wearied, beneath a spreading banyan tree, and Yudhishthira bade Nakula fetch water from a tank.

Nakula went to the tank, and prepared to draw water. But, as he did so, a voice from the air said, "Be not over-bold; but answer first my questions, and then drink and carry hence." But Nakula, being athirst, heeded not the voice; he drank of the cool water, and straightway fell dead.

Seeing that Nakula tarried long, Yudhishthira sent his twin-brother, Sahadeva, to hasten matters. Great was the grief of Sahadeva when, on reaching the tank, he saw his brother lying dead; but, being sore athirst, he ran to the water to drink. Again the voice bade him pause and first answer certain questions. But Sahadeva would not stay; he drank, and, like Nakula, in a trice he fell dead. When he came not, Yudhishthira sent Arjuna to learn the cause of delay.

The great warrior was much moved when he saw

"The Voice came to Him"

his brethren lying dead, and he made ready his bow to shoot; but he saw no man to strike. Then came the voice from the air, saying, "Why dost thou essay to take by force the forbidden water? Answer first certain questions, and then shalt thou drink and carry hence." In hot anger, Arjuna replied, "Show thyself, if thou wouldst hinder me! My arrows shall teach thee not to speak thus!"

So saying he shot arrows thick as rain in every direction, but to no purpose. Then, overcome with thirst, he went and drank; and he too fell dead.

Then Yudhishthira, in great anxiety, sent Bhima to inquire the cause of the long delay. Bhima departed, and soon found his three brothers lying dead by the water-side. Wrathfully he took thought of fighting; but first he would seek to slake his thirst. To him also came the voice, bidding him first answer the questions. But Bhima heeded not the voice, and, without answering, he drank of the water, and straightway he fell prone.

In the end, Yudhishthira went, perforce, himself to learn what was amiss. There, by the side of the tank, he found his four brothers lying, to all appearance, dead. Long and woefully he lamented over them, questioning bitterly why warriors so upright and valiant should be thus unworthily reft of life. In the end, he too approached the water; but as he was in the act of stepping in, the voice came to him also, bidding him refrain till he had answered that which should be asked of him.

Now Yudhishthira was wise in counsel; and, instead of wrathfully disregarding the voice of one whom he could not see, he inquired, wonderingly the name of the questioner, if perchance it should be some god.

The voice answered, "I am a Yaksha, and by me thy brothers were slain. I bade them forbear, but they heeded not, and sought to drink in my despite. And thou too, O King, drink not hastily, if thou lovest life; but first answer my questions, and then take to drink if thou wilt."

Then answered Yudhishthira, "Far be it from me, O Yaksha, to slight thy command! First ask, as thou sayest, what thou wilt, and I shall answer as best I may."

"Say, then," said the Yaksha, "what causes the sun to rise and to set; who are its attendants, and in what is it established?"

"Brahma," replied Yudhishthira, "causes the sun to rise, and Dharma causes it to set; the gods are its attendants, and in truth it is established."

"What," said the Yaksha, "is that which closes not its eyes in sleep; that which stirs not at birth; that which has no heart; and that which swells by its own force?"

"A fish," answered Yudhishthira, "closes not its eyes in sleep; an egg stirs not at birth; a stone is that which has no heart; and rivers swell by their own force."

The Yaksha asked, "Who is the invincible enemy of man? What is his permanent disease? Who is held to be holy, and who unholy?"

Then answered Yudhishthira, "Anger is the foe right hard to vanquish, and covetousness the permanent disease. He who is set on the welfare of all is held to be holy, and unholy he who is pitiless."

"Tell me quickly," then asked the Yaksha, "who go to everlasting hell?"

And Yudhishthira answered, "The man who, having himself invited a mendicant Brahman, afterwards says, 'I have nothing'; also, those who impute falsehood to the Vedas and other Scriptures and to Brahmans; also, one who, though known to be wealthy, denies it and spends naught in charity—all these go to everlasting hell."

With these and many other hard questions did the Yaksha ply Yudhishthira, touching all matters in all three worlds, from the least to the greatest. Other men might well have failed through ignorance or impatience; but Yudhishthira was both wise and patient, and he answered every question wittingly, without anger or mistake. Then at length the Yaksha said, "Thou hast shown thyself faultless in all; therefore thy brothers may live again."

With that word of the Yaksha, the four brethren on the ground rose up, and all their hunger and thirst departed in a twinkling. But Yudhishthira was fain to clear the matter up, and he said—

"I would ask yet again who thou art—no Yaksha, methinks, art thou. These brethren of mine are mighty warriors, and such as they fall not before the common sort. Haply thou art one of the Vasus or Maruts—I pray thee, tell us!"

Thus urged, the voice answered Yudhishthira, "Know, then, that I am thine own sire, Dharma, the god of Duty, and I have thus dealt with thee to prove thee, and thou hast acquitted thyself right well in the trial."

Then the god granted to Yudhishthira various boons of his own choosing; and the Pandavas departed happily to their dwelling again. Among other things that the god had granted was this: that—as they were now come to the time when they would have to pass a year in disguise—they should be unrecognisable, whatever disguise they might assume.

IV

The thirteenth year being now upon them, the Pandavas repaired to the kingdom of Virata. Yudhishthira gave himself out to be a professional dicer; for one of the sages had endowed him, during the sojourn in the forest, with perfect skill in dicing. Bhima posed as a cook; Arjuna, as a teacher of music and dancing; Nakula and Sahadeva, as groom and herdsman respectively; and Draupadi, as a maid-servant.

On going before the king to ask for employment, the monarch doubted somewhat of their appearance, which, he thought, was that rather of kings than of servants. However, they answered all questions discreetly, and were given the employment that they had desired.

Their great strength and valour, however, could not long remain hid. Bhima overthrew a mighty wrestler, and afterwards contended successfully with wild beasts in the arena. Furthermore, when Kichaka, King Virata's chief commander, vexed Draupadi with proposals of marriage, and treated her with great violence when she refused, Bhima lay in wait for him when he was alone, and slew him in a desperate combat without arms.

On hearing of Kichaka's death, certain of Virata's foes thought good to make an invasion. They invited the Kauravas to assist them, and the two armies forthwith raided Virata's cattle. The Pandava brethren offered their services for fighting, and through their assistance the Kauravas and their allies were defeated. The news of victory was taken back by Uttara, the king's son, whom Arjuna persuaded to conceal the share which the Pandavas had in the victory. Uttara modestly told the king that the success was due not to himself, but to the son of a god, who was now invisible, but would soon reappear.

Anon, the year having now run out, the Pandavas came forth in kingly guise, and announced to King Virata the truth about themselves. Virata was delighted, and offered Arjuna his daughter Uttará in marriage. Arjuna declined for himself, but accepted the maiden on behalf of his son Abhimanyu. The wedding was celebrated with great pomp, and Krishna himself attended with a mighty following.

The Pandavas now consulted King Virata and others as to what course they should take; for they had endured much wrong, and it might well be their duty as warriors to seek vengeance in war. Krishna and his half-brother, Balarama by name, besought them to seek their end by peaceful means, and forthwith departed for Dwaraka, not wishing to take part in hostilities.

Arjuna and Duryodhana, the chief warriors on either side, then set off to Dwaraka, to get Krishna's advice. Krishna offered to help both parties, and gave the twain the choice between a vast army, given by himself, and his own counsel during the war, though he himself would take no part in the actual fighting. Arjuna chose Krishna, while Duryodhana preferred the army.

To compass a peaceful arrangement, Drupada, the father-in-law of the Pandavas, sent his priest as ambassador to Dhritarashtra. Bhishma, the venerable half-brother of Vyasa, acting as counsellor of the king's party, advised peace. But Karna—who, though half-brother to the Pandavas, sided with the Kurus, because his mother had abandoned him as a child—said that nothing would be yielded to threats, and that the Pandavas ought to live as simple subjects of King Dhritarashtra.

The old king then sent his own charioteer, Sanjaya, as ambassador to the Pandavas. Sanjaya spoke of the might of the Kauravas, and of the short-lived nature of even the best that human triumphs can bring. Yudhishthira, on his part, dwelt specially on the surpassing prowess of Arjuna, and on the Kshatriya's duty to fight. When he again sought the advice of Krishna, the god said that peace was indeed to be desired, but it was not the mark of a warrior to avoid fighting. Yudhishthira asked that only a small allowance of territory should be given them, and they would be content.

On the return of Sanjaya to Dhritarashtra's court, Bhishma and the wiser counsellors strongly advised the king to deal kindly with the Pandavas. Duryodhana, however, was obstinate in his pride, and would heed nothing, not even the rebuke of his own mother Gandhari, who foretold his humiliation and defeat at the hands of Bhima.

Willing to make yet one more attempt at conciliating their enemies, the five brethren persuaded Krishna himself to go on an embassy to the Kauravas. This Krishna consented to do, on the ground that, if Duryodhana refused such high counsel, his destruction would be wholly deserved.

Krishna, therefore, set out with goodly omens, and Dhritarashtra, on hearing of his approach, proposed to welcome him with due honour. Duryodhana spoke scornfully of the proposal, and shamelessly suggested that Krishna should be seized and made prisoner.

When, on the day after his arrival, Krishna made his entry into the assembly, heavenly sages were seen descending from the sky to take part in the council. When Krishna had spoken long and wisely, these sages added words of their own to the same end, showing, by many a well-chosen tale of olden time, the woeful results of obstinacy and pride. Most of the Kuru leaders were fain to yield to this wise persuasion; but Duryodhana was proof against all. When Krishna pleaded further with him personally, and Dhritarashtra, Bhishma, and others urged him to listen, he spurned their entreaties with scornful words, vowing that not an inch of territory would ever be given up to the Pandavas. Even his mother Gandhari, being summoned to the council, failed to abate his violence; and he departed in great wrath, to devise plans for laying hands on Krishna himself.

On Duryodhana's departure, Krishna revealed to the assembly his divine form, showing himself to be the source and lord of all; then, after receiving the worship of those present, he resumed his human guise and departed.

Ere he returned to the Pandavas, Krishna sought to win Karna to their cause. Karna was, indeed, born of the same mother, by a different father, before she wedded Pandu. But he replied that she had disowned him in infancy, and that the charioteer and his wife who had brought him up bound him to the Kaurava party. And when his mother herself sought him out alone, as he performed his devotions on the bank of the Ganges, Karna had no other answer even for her; but he promised that he would not fight to the death with any of the five brothers save Arjuna. So they embraced, and parted.

Forthwith the leaders of either party addressed themselves to marshalling their forces for the fray. Among the chiefs on the Pandava side, besides the brethren themselves, were Drupada and his son Dhrishtadyumna, Virata, and Sikhandin.

At the request of Duryodhana, the chief command of the Kuru host was taken by the aged Bhishma. He had boundless knowledge of war, and was of great wisdom in all manner of affairs. When asked by Duryodhana to estimate the worth of the Pandava leaders, he spoke highly of many of them, and averred that Arjuna was without a peer in either army. Still, he boasted of his own skill in war, and the Kurus welcomed his appointment to the lordship of the host with mighty acclamation.

But Bhishma spoke contemptuously of Karna; and that great warrior was filled with wrath, and charged Bhishma with sowing seeds of discord among the leaders when union was most needed.

On the side of the Kurus there fought also Drona, the instructor of the two families, who still held the Pandavas in high esteem. Other great chiefs were his son, Aswatthaman, Kripa, and Salya, king of Madra.

The two armies prepared for the strife with equal confidence. Most of the Kuru lords thought to see the Pandavas destroyed in a few days; while Arjuna professed that, with his wondrous weapons, and with Krishna for his charioteer and adviser, he could overthrow all his foes in a twinkling.

V

Who can fittingly recount in a few short pages the tale of the mighty battle, or, rather, days of battle, to which the old Sanskrit poem gives four times the bulk of Homer's Iliad?

The nature, too, of the combat, as described, was such that Homer's heroes would seem mere pigmies or triflers, if compared with those who fought on Kurukshetra. Many of these were endued with extraordinary powers of divine origin. Some were the offspring of gods; others of demi-gods, Danavas, Rakshasas, or the like. Among the weapons wielded were some surpassing any that human skill could forge, or human wit devise—weapons by which fire, water, or clouds might be created on a sudden, or hosts of opponents made unconscious or cut off in an instant. Some of these dread fighters, thus dreadfully armed, could spring aloft in the air and thence o'erwhelm their foes; at other moments, when weary and hard pressed, they could become invisible, and thus escape the violence of reviving enemies. These were warriors to whom mere multitude was nought—in their conquering fury they could overbear scores—nay, myriads of meaner breed; while they strove in their own unaided might against horses, cars, and elephants, and sent them to destruction by thousands.

In numbers, too, the armies of Kuru and Pandava that strove for mastery were such as to make the largest hosts of sober history seem as trifling as the parties in a village brawl.

While the hosts were thus being marshalled, Vyasa, the grandsire of Kurus and Pandavas, offered his blind son, the King Dhritarashtra, the power of sight during the battle. But Dhritarashtra, fearing to look on the slaughter of his kindred, preferred to remain blind. Instead of this boon, therefore, Vyasa bestowed on Sanjaya, the king's charioteer, the gift of being invulnerable and of seeing all that took place at any point by day or night. And perchance it was well for Dhritarashtra that he saw not, if he feared to look on slaughter; for dread portents were manifest both in the sky and on earth, foreshowing the death of multitudes.

Sanjaya forthwith discoursed to the king of many things, past, present, and future. Krishna, likewise, as charioteer to Arjuna, had to encourage his friend. For Arjuna, gazing on the hosts mustering for battle, remembered that among the chiefs against him were kinsmen, friends, and teachers; his heart began to fail him, and his senses were numbed with dismay. Thereon Krishna commenced a famous discourse, known as the Bhagavad-gita, or Song of the Blessed; in which he began by encouraging Arjuna to do his duty as a warrior, forgetful of human ties. The soul, he said, slays not, nor is slain; death, so called, is but a change of body. Afterwards, he held forth to Arjuna on the duty of faith, and revealed himself in his divine form; whereby Arjuna was lifted up to an ecstasy of adoration and praise. Then, being comforted, he took the great bow Gandiva, and prepared to do battle.

In this hour of preparation, Yudhishthira did not forget the respect due to his elders and instructors. He went forward toward the Kaurava host in suppliant guise, and with much reverence paid his respects to Bhishma, Drona, and others. This worthy act of Yudhishthira moved both friends and foes to deep admiration; and Bhishma himself said that this reverent conduct had made Yudhishthira's victory certain.

The two armies then joined battle with the roar of a mighty tempest. Day after day the strife raged unspeakably. Millions of the common sort perished before the onslaught of the chiefs of either party. Many, too, were the encounters between the leaders themselves, in which at one time the Pandava, at another the Kaurava, would have the greater honour. Yet of the chiefest warriors none was struck down till the tenth day of fighting.

On that day it came to pass that Bhishma himself, who had destroyed thousands and myriads of the Pandava armies, was stricken down. He died not, it is true, on the selfsame day; indeed, the manner of his final passing was strange beyond the common. On this tenth day Arjuna, who had more than once before fought against Bhishma with wondrous valour, but without in any way overcoming him, attacked him once more with surpassing fury. Bhishma, weary of fighting and of life itself, fought bravely indeed, as became him; but he was overborne. In the end, he was so pierced with the countless arrows rained upon him by Arjuna and those with him, that there remained not on the old warrior's body a space of two fingers' breadth unpierced. He had, however, the power to delay his death till a time when the sun stood in an auspicious quarter. So he bade his friends lay him down; and the fighters on either hand forebore their strife, and drew near to behold this strange sight of the aged Bhishma thus couched, as it were, upon a bed of arrows. His head hanging down, Arjuna made him a pillow of three arrows, and drew forth water from the ground to slake his thirst.

In this strange plight he lay for many a day, while the others returned to wage wild warfare to the end.

Bhishma being laid aside, Drona was chosen by Duryodhana and Karna to lead the Kauravas. Duryodhana besought Drona to take Yudhishthira alive, and Drona therefore tried to draw away Arjuna from Yudhishthira's side, that the eldest Pandava might be left unprotected. But Arjuna first gave charge concerning the protection of Yudhishthira, and then fell on those who sought to draw him away. After a great combat, he slew one of the most noted of the Kaurava warriors, Bhagadatta by name; but in another part of the field Abhimanyu, Arjuna's own son, after doing deeds of might, was set on by Karna and many car-warriors, and perished.

Great was the woe of the Pandavas on Abhimanyu's death. To cheer them, Vyasa suddenly appeared, and with many a wise tale, showing how not even the bravest can avoid death, he comforted Yudhishthira and encouraged him to continue the struggle.

Arjuna then vowed to slay Jayadratha, King of the Sindhus, against whom Abhimanyu had been fighting when he met his end. It was this Jayadratha who had formerly carried off Draupadi; after which, by devotions and austerities, he gained the power of being able to stand against any Pandava save Arjuna only. Thus it came to pass that, although he was guarded by many of the bravest Kuru warriors, it availed him not when Arjuna drew near to fight against him; bravely, indeed, he fought, but Arjuna vanquished him and cut off his head.

On this day Bhima also did valiantly, and many of Dhritarashtra's sons did he send to Yama's realm. He fought for a space with Drona, till Karna came up to defend his lord. Bhima and Karna then strove furiously, each obtaining some advantage in turn; then Arjuna came to Bhima's aid, and Karna withdrew from the battle.

Aswatthaman, the son of Drona, showed great prowess on this day. It therefore came to the mind of Krishna to advise the Pandavas to spread a false report of Aswatthaman's death, so that Drona might lose heart and cease to fight. Bhima then slew an elephant named Aswatthaman, and told Drona that Aswatthaman was dead. Drona believed him not, and asked Yudhishthira concerning the report. Now Yudhishthira, as became the son of the god Dharma himself, had ever been known far and wide, by both friend and foe, as the foremost of truth-tellers. So pure was his spirit, that his car in battle touched not the earth, but drove a hand's breadth above it. But in this hour, persuaded by one who claimed to be Lord of all, Yudhishthira answered Drona that Aswatthaman was indeed dead; but he added the word "elephant" under his breath. Then the car of Yudhishthira touched the earth like others; but Drona, filled with despair, gave up the fight, and, sitting in his car wrapt in devotion, was slain by Dhrishtadyumna, who cut off his head, and cast it before the Kaurava host.

Hearing of his father's death, Aswatthaman assailed the Pandava army with fury, and by means of a mystical weapon he ravaged their ranks as with fire. Arjuna, however, had also command of certain celestial weapons, and with these the violence of Aswatthaman was stayed. But he had vowed to destroy the whole Pandava host, and what came of the vow shall be told hereafter; while the lie that Yudhishthira had told, though told by the counsel of a god, laid up for him in the future a cruel woe.

VI

Drona being dead, the Kauravas chose for their leader Karna, the half-brother of the Pandavas. He straightway went forth to the battle, with Salya, king of the Madras, as his charioteer, and entered into conflict with Yudhishthira himself. The Pandava prince at first struck down his foeman with an arrow; but Karna, recovering, showered arrows on Yudhishthira, who was with difficulty rescued by his brethren, his steeds being cut down and his charioteer slain.

When the princes returned to the fight, Duh-sasana, who had formerly dragged Draupadi by the hair into the hall of assembly, boldly withstood Bhima, and at first wounded him sorely. But Bhima was not a whit daunted, and after a grievous combat Duh-sasana was slain; and Bhima, according to his vow, tore open his enemy's breast and drank his blood.

More awful still was the mortal strife of Karna and Arjuna, who made at one another like mad elephants. Each hurled weapon after weapon on the other, and their arrows flew in clouds. At last the wheel of Karna's chariot began to sink in the earth; and Karna knew that his end was nigh: for a Brahman whom he had offended long ago had cursed him, saying that in his hour of need his chariot wheel would sink in the earth. He strove to raise it, shaking the very earth and the seven seas with the effort. Then Arjuna pierced him with a deadly shaft, and, ere he could regain his car, struck off his head. From the headless corpse there flew forth light; for Karna's father was the Sun-god, and to him the light returned. The Pandavas blew their horns, but despair filled the hearts of the Kurus.

Next day, Salya was appointed commander, and a frightful combat ensued between him and Bhima. The blows of their clubs crashed forth like thunder, and each, sore stricken by the other, withdrew for a space. But anon Yudhishthira, supported by his brethren on either hand, bestirred himself, for all his mildness, to fight against Salya. The Madra monarch bore himself right stoutly against this fearful onslaught; but in vain. His attack was foiled by Yudhishthira's comrades, and he fell beneath a magic dart from the prince's hand.

One Kuru leader after another had thus perished in the devouring fray, and the Kuru host, bereft of its chiefs, now became a prey to the fury of the Pandavas. Myriads and myriads were swiftly destroyed, till, of that vast army, there remained but four persons—Duryodhana, Aswatthaman, Kripa, and Kritavarman.

Duryodhana took his departure alone, and coming, in the course of his journeying, to a lake, he entered its waters, and by magical powers caused them to enclose him as in a chamber, and so rested for a space. The other three followed Duryodhana, and on reaching the lake aroused him and called on him to carry on the struggle to the end. Duryodhana answered that he would surely do so after he had rested.

News of their doings, however, came to the Pandavas through hunters. Bhima, overjoyed, rewarded the

"Bhima hurled his Mace with Fury" 216

informers liberally, and Yudhishthira, on reaching the lake, called on Duryodhana to come forth and do a warrior's duty. When Duryodhana spoke of his weariness, Yudhishthira taunted him with cowardice, and stung by this and other taunts Duryodhana at length came forth, having offered to fight all the Pandavas, one after another. Bhima joyfully accepted the challenge, and the two warriors prepared to do battle with the mace, for each excelled in the use of this tremendous weapon.

Their conflict was preceded by dire omens in earth and sky; the blows fell with the noise of thunder, and sparks flew from their maces as they clashed together. Each in turn felled his enemy to the ground; but though thus grievously stricken, both on head and body, neither gave place sufficiently to allow the other to make an end of him.

While they thus fought, Arjuna asked Krishna how Bhima might in the end prevail. Krishna replied that, as Duryodhana was full of deceit and wickedness, Bhima might well use unfair means. He reminded Arjuna how Bhima had sworn to break Duryodhana's thigh; this, therefore, though it was reckoned a foul blow in such fights, it was time for him to do. Arjuna then struck his hand on his thigh, so that Bhima saw it; and Bhima, remembering his vow, hurled his mace with fury, and smashed both of Duryodhana's thighs. Down fell the stricken warrior, while many cried shame on Bhima for the blow. Duryodhana, too, raising himself painfully on his arms, reviled Krishna, and charged him with unfair dealing throughout the war. Yudhishthira strove to console Duryodhana by reminding him that the blow was dealt in fulfilment of a vow; while Krishna sought to justify double-dealing in no very godlike manner.

The Pandavas now entered the Kaurava camp, where they found none but aged men, women, and the like. Dhritarashtra and Gandhari were approached by Krishna, in Hastinapura, and were forced to confess that things had but fallen out even as they themselves had warned Duryodhana, and that the Pandavas had gained the victory because they were in the right.

The surviving Kuru leaders, Aswatthaman, Kripa, and Kritavarman, paid a visit to Duryodhana, who lay yet living, though bathed in blood, and then departed southward. Hearing the shouts of the Pandava army, they resorted to a thick wood, and took shelter under a great banyan-tree. Foredone with toil, Kripa and Kritavarman fell asleep; but Aswatthaman sat wakeful, and nursed his wrath. While he thus brooded, he noticed that crows in thousands roosted in the wide branches of the tree. But even as he watched them, there came a mighty owl of grim aspect, brown-eyed, with huge beak and talons. It slid softly through the air towards the spreading branches, and fell with fury on the sleeping crows. Of some it tare the wings, and it rent off the heads of others. Anon, the tree and the ground beneath it were covered with the corpses of the crows, and the owl gloated over them.

Then Drona's son thought in his heart, "The bird has taught me a lesson well suited to my need, and the time is ripe. Fighting lawfully, we are doomed; but by craft one may achieve success and huge slaughter of foes."

Thereon he roused his two companions and set forth his plan. They counselled him to rest first; but Aswatthaman, burning to avenge his father's death, could not bear the thought of delay. Nor would he grant that there was shame in slaying foes in their sleep, for the Pandavas themselves—so said Aswatthaman—had dealt unfairly in many ways. Among such deeds he recalled specially the slaying of his father Drona by Dhrishtadyumna; for Drona abandoning himself to his fate, had laid aside his arms and given himself up to devotion when the fatal moment came.

Thus bent on the deed of vengeance, Aswatthaman advanced towards the camp of his enemies. Ere he entered, there met him an awful figure, none other than the god Siva. After attacking him for a time, Aswatthaman perceived with whom he strove, and worshipped the god with a song of praise. Thereon appeared the dread attendants of the god-goblins, fiends, and divers beasts of prey. While these celebrated a fearful orgy, the god came forward again, and encouraged Drona's son in his enterprise, and gave him a goodly weapon. Attended by the dread myrmidons of the awful deity, the Kuru chieftain entered the camp, having bidden the other two to guard the gates, lest any should escape.

First Aswatthaman sought out Dhrishtadyumna, wakened him rudely, and kicked him to death. When the Pandava guards surrounded the slayer, he cut them in pieces with the mystic weapon.

The greater part thought themselves the victims of a fiend's attack, and the strength to resist went from them. Others were filled with delusion, and slew their fellows. All the rest of the night the slaughter lasted; and when morning rose, Aswatthaman left the Pandava camp as he had found it—silent.

He then gladdened Kripa and Kritavarman with the tale of his success. They then repaired together to Duryodhana's resting-place, and revived his dying ears with the news of the slaughter. Thereon Duryodhana, having congratulated them, gave up the ghost, and his spirit departed to Swarga; for, though cruel and rude, he had been a stout warrior, and, as such, he was to obtain the reward of those who died a warrior's death.

Now it chanced that the Pandava brethren themselves, with Draupadi, were not in the camp on the fatal night, but rested somewhat apart. For they had been counselled to take heed to themselves in some such way, lest the last efforts of the Kurus should reach them even in the hour of victory. Of those in the camp there escaped one, the charioteer of Dhrishtadyumna, who bare tidings to Yudhishthira; and he straightway fell senseless on hearing the news. Coming to himself, he went to survey the woeful scene, and there again, beholding the mangled remains of those who had served him so well, he was stricken with grief, and swooned away.

Scarcely, too, could the old king Dhritarashtra be consoled for the loss of all his sons. His father, the sage Vyasa, sought to comfort him by many arguments. Death, he said, was the portion of all alike; death met valiantly was better than dishonourable life; while Duryodhana and his brothers had really drawn destruction on themselves by their many misdeeds. Somewhat comforted, the king abandoned the desire to part with life; but when his charioteer Sanjaya bade him prepare to celebrate the funeral rites of his offspring, his grief returned, and he fell senseless to the ground. Revived by the ministrations of his friends, he went forth with Gandhari to the scene of the conflict, and on his way met Aswatthaman and his comrades, who shared in the lamentations of the sorrowing parents, while they told of the slaughter of the sleeping Pandavas. They then departed, lest the five brethren should come upon them.

Anon Yudhishthira and the others arrived, and prepared to meet the king. Dhritarashtra reluctantly embraced Yudhishthira, but purposed in his heart to crush to death Bhima, the slayer of so many of his sons; for the old king, despite his age and blindness, had well-nigh measureless strength. Krishna, however, knew his purpose, and presented for the king's embrace an iron image. This the king crushed to pieces, though greatly to his own hurt; then he confessed his treacherous intent and wept aloud, thinking that he had slain Bhima. Krishna told him the truth, and the king then embraced Bhima and the others peaceably.

Gandhari would not at first receive the brethren in peace, and was fain to curse them; such was her wrath that it was like to scorch their very bodies. However, in the end she was appeased, and spake kindly to them. But when, by special power granted by Vyasa, she beheld the dreadful battlefield from end to end, her misery broke forth afresh, and she cursed Krishna himself for not having prevented such general destruction. Krishna replied that the mother's curse would not fall to the ground; beneath its weight all his own sons, the whole Yadava race, would perish.

The funeral rites of the slain were then performed, and it was then that the Pandavas learned for the first time from their mother that Karna, their foe, was her own son, and therefore their half-brother.

Deep had been the grief of Yudhishthira already over the destruction of his kinsfolk; it was now redoubled when he learned that Karna and Arjuna, his slayer, were brothers. Forthwith he declared his intention of departing to the forests, to spend the rest of his days as a hermit. To this his brothers opposed many an argument, and Krishna seconded their appeal. Finally, Yudhishthira yielded to their words, and entered Hastinapura in triumph; but, with due humility, he caused Dhritarashtra and Gandhari to be borne in front of his car. He was then installed as king, having commanded, however, that the same honour should be paid to Dhritarashtra as before. Appointments were made for the wise conduct of government, and Yudhishthira's rule bade fair to be in every way honourable and glorious.

In these days the brethren went with Krishna to the battlefield, to visit the stricken Bhishma, who, as was told before, reclined, yet living, on a support formed by the countless arrows with which he was pierced. Marvellous indeed was this strange prolonging of life; yet even more wonderful was it that, in this dying attitude, he had still strength to pour forth instruction to his hearers on every subject that could interest them or in any way concern them. In the end, having thus traversed almost every theme relating to heaven and earth, to man and beast, with numerous tales to illustrate the many precepts enjoined, Bhishma advised Yudhishthira to return to Hastinapura, and to do honour to the gods and the shades of his ancestors. At a further time appointed, when the sun had entered an auspicious part of his course, Yudhishthira rejoined Bhishma, who, in the presence of Dhritarashtra and the Pandavas, yielded up his spirit, amid heavenly music and rain of flowers.

When his funeral rites had been performed, Yudhishthira again nearly yielded to the crushing weight of sorrow upon sorrow; for Bhishma, though ranged against Yudhishthira in battle, had ever been to him a beloved kinsman and a revered teacher. But Vyasa and Krishna bade him rouse himself and celebrate the famous Horse-sacrifice, whereby princes with supreme dominion were said to be purified from sin.

For this sacrifice, it was necessary that the horse chosen for the offering should be set free for one year to wander over the earth whither it would. Following it went the monarch's champion, whose duty it was to demand submission to his liege lord from all into whose domains the horse wandered. This high office was given to Arjuna, whose skill in war surpassed that of all the brethren. As it was the duty of the warrior caste to fight whenever the slightest occasion offered itself, it need scarce be said that attendance on the horse brought with it a full measure of warfare. It were idle here to tell of all Arjuna's adventures and combats; they were many and strenuous; nay, once he was so deeply stricken in fight, that he fell insensible, to all appearance dead, and was only restored by the virtue of a magic gem. But he triumphed over all hardships, and in the end returned with the horse to Hastinapura, where Yudhishthira prepared a pageant of infinite costliness and magnificence to give him welcome.

Lavish were the gifts of the king to the Brahmans who were to perform the sacrifice, and unbounded was his largesse of food to all who had need thereof. The horse was slain, and Yudhishthira and his brothers smelled the savour of the offering, and were thereby purified from their faults. Again was made a distribution of measureless wealth in gold and jewels, both to Brahmans and, when these were satisfied, to others also. Parikshit, the grandson of Arjuna, whose father Abhimanyu had been slain in the fray, was proclaimed heir-apparent, and the great ceremonial came to an end.

VII

Yudhishthira, thus installed in his kingdom, ruled wisely and happily for fifteen years. In the main, all ill-feeling between Kurus and Pandavas had been laid aside; Draupadi was to Gandhari as a daughter, and Dhritarashtra received every honour from Yudhishthira. But betwixt the old king and Bhima the enmity lived on, each contriving ill against the other in many ways. At length Dhritarashtra gave out his resolve to go with his wife to the forests, and there to end his days as a hermit. To this Yudhishthira was unwilling to agree; but his consent was given at last, and the old king and queen went forth, clad in garments of skins and bark-cloth, the mother of the Pandavas going with them, despite all the entreaties of her sons.

So, amid great commotion and lament, these elders of the two families walked forth, clad in the humble garments of ascetics. Arrived at the forest, they lived the austere life of hermits, feeding but rarely, and even then only on water and the scantiest of other food. Such was the rigour of their penances that, when Yudhishthira and the others set out for a visit to the elders, these were found reduced to such frailty of body that they seemed but skin and bone, scarce sufficient to retain the vital flame. The Pandava princes saluted their aged relatives with all reverence, carrying for them their jars of water; and withal the meeting was one of great friendliness. Then, by his mystic powers, Vyasa called forth a vision of the slain relatives of those present; and thereon, with great uproar, there came forth from the Ganges the shades of all the lordly dead who fell on either side. All talked harmoniously among themselves and with those on the earth before them, and the night was passed with much happiness. Then the shades plunged again into the waters of Ganges, and many of the widows of those warriors cast themselves into the stream, hoping thus to rejoin their husbands.

Some years later, the forest wherein the old king and those with him dwelt took fire, and for weakness they could not escape; thus all the elders perished in the flames. It was told Yudhishthira that they had not desired to be saved, as the time was ripe for their departure to the abodes of the blest. The Pandavas, deeply grieved, repaired to the spot; oblations were made to the shades of the deceased, and, Yudhishthira having performed the chief office in the funeral rites, they returned to the capital.

There remained now but one great happening to fill up the tale of sorrows which, despite the glory of their victory, could scarce fail to cloud the happiness of the Pandava brethren.

It has been told how Krishna, the hero who passed for a god, dwelt in a great city, Dwaraka by name, not far from the sea, and there ruled over a people consisting of his own sons, of whom there was a great multitude. It has also been told how it was fated that all this people, the Yadava race, should perish; and it came to pass on this wise.

Six and thirty years had passed since the dread battle of Kurukshetra, when strange and awful portents were seen by King Yudhishthira, and the hearts of the Pandavas were bowed with fear. And rightly so; for anon came tidings that the whole Yadava race had perished.

These Yadavas, though sprung from one reputed a god, were in no wise distinguished by piety or good conduct. They were not above playing a foolish jest on a company of sages, who, in return, uttered a curse foretelling the speedy destruction of the Yadavas. The latter on other occasions also insulted

Brahmans, and were all too ready to indulge in strong drink to excess, whence arose quarrels many and violent.

The utterance of this curse was followed by dire omens. Krishna, perceiving that the overthrow of his people was at hand, returned his divine weapon to the skies, and abandoned his chariot, which the steeds bore away in wondrous fashion over the waves of Ocean.

The Yadavas being now gathered at Prabhasa on the seashore, for the purpose of bathing in the sacred waters, much feasting and revelry took place. In this, none was more forward than Balarama, Krishna's half-brother, who was also held to be half-divine. As the Yadavas feasted and drank, many became heated with wine, and hot words began to pass. Kritavarman, one of the four Kauravas who had wrought destruction upon the sleeping Pandava host, being present at the banquet, was grievously insulted and taunted with having slain sleeping foes. He replied fiercely, on which Satyaki, who had insulted him, ran upon him and smote off his head. Others then fell on Satyaki, and he in turn was slain. Thereon the strife became general, and Krishna himself, taking part, slew many with blades of grass which turned to weapons in his hands. Son slew father, and father son, with blades of grass turned to clubs; they fell as insects fall in a flame; none had wit for flight. Thus perished the Yadavas.

It was now time that Krishna and Balarama should quit their mortal state and return to the abode of the gods. Krishna therefore sent messengers to bid Arjuna come with speed. He then repaired to the forest, and there found his half-brother already sunk in devotional exercise. From Balarama's mouth there issued a mighty snake; for the deity that was incarnate in him was Sesha, the great World-serpent. Krishna then addressed himself likewise to devotional meditation, and sat down with his left leg and foot across his right thigh. In the foot thus exposed he was shot with an arrow from the bow of a hunter, who had mistaken Krishna's movements for those of a deer; for it was fated that Krishna should suffer death by a wound in his foot. He comforted the hunter, who was overcome with fear, and then ascended to heaven with great splendour.

Arjuna then arrived, and sorrowfully greeted Vasudeva, Krishna's aged father, and Krishna's wives, together with those of the slain warriors. Vasudeva told Arjuna that Krishna had forewarned them that Dwaraka would be overflowed by Ocean after his departure; Arjuna therefore commanded all who remained there to gather their gear together and prepare to depart with him to Indraprastha. The funeral rites of the Yadavas were performed, and the journey began. Barbarians attacked the travellers on their way, and Arjuna found, to his dismay, that his bow Gandiva and the inexhaustible quivers would no longer serve their purpose as formerly. Many of the ladies of the party were thus carried off; and Arjuna, seeing in these things the hand of Fate, forebore to strive.

Having seen to the settlement of those who remained, Arjuna in deep woe sought the hermitage of his grandsire Vyasa. The sage learned from him the woeful tale of the Yadavas, but comforted Arjuna with the assurance that all this sorrow only portended the close of their earthly trials; for the Pandavas, said he, had now achieved their great life's work, and it only remained for them to depart and be exalted in heaven.

Thus instructed, Arjuna departed to Hastinapura, and told Yudhishthira all that had passed.

VIII

When he heard of the utter downfall of the Yadavas, Yudhishthira felt that his hour was come. Arjuna and the others thought with him, and they resolved forthwith to set out on pilgrimage.

Parikshit was anointed king in Hastinapura, and Vajra, the only one left of the Yadavas, was appointed to reign at Indraprastha. Yudhishthira and his brothers performed the funeral rites of the slain, and gave great feasts in honour of the holy sages who were present at the ceremony. Then they laid aside their princely ornaments and put on raiment of bark-cloth, and prepared for departure. The citizens sought to turn them from their purpose, but they would not be persuaded. Loud wept the women as they saw the five brethren and Draupadi setting forth, as in the day when they were conquered in dicing. They, however, went forth cheerfully; and as they departed a dog joined himself to their company.

Fasting much, and wrapt in devotion, they journeyed first eastward over many lands. In front went Yudhishthira, with Bhima next; then followed Arjuna, then Nakula and Sahadeva; and last came lotus-eyed Draupadi, best of women. Behind came the dog; no other attendant had they.

Anon they came to the Red Ocean. There they saw the god of Fire over against them, huge as a hill. He bade Arjuna give up to him the bow Gandiva and the inexhaustible quivers; for thus far Arjuna had not brought himself to part with these. Agni said that they had been taken of old from Varuna, and to Varuna they must now be returned, for Arjuna could have no use for them henceforth. So Arjuna cast the bow and quivers into the waters, and forthwith Agni disappeared.

Then the Pandavas, after much journeying in various directions, beheld, as they moved westward, the city of Dwaraka with the ocean washing over it. Northward then they went, desiring to make the circuit of the earth, and saw the mighty mountains of Himavan. Crossing these, they beheld a wilderness of sand, and Meru, prince of mountains, afar off.

Then, as they sped onward, on a sudden Draupadi fell to earth. Beholding her fall, Bhima said to the good king, "Our princess has done no wrong! Say now, wherefore has Draupadi fallen to the ground?"

And Yudhishthira answered: "She loved Arjuna too well, and she now reaps the fruit thereof." And so, not looking back on her, he went steadfastly onward.

Then fell, in like manner, the wise Sahadeva; and, seeing him fall, Bhima asked the king: "Wherefore is he fallen, who was so humble among us all?"

Then answered Yudhishthira: "For this fault is he

fallen, that he reckoned none so wise as himself." And leaving Sahadeva, Yudhishthira pressed on with his brothers and the dog.

Then Nakula, having seen with grief the fall of Draupadi and Sahadeva, dropped down. Again Bhima asked Yudhishthira: "Why is Nakula laid low, our upright brother, unsurpassed in beauty?"

And Yudhishthira made answer: "Our brother Nakula, thoughtful and upright, said in his heart, 'None is my peer in beauty; nay, I am beyond all.' Therefore is he fallen; and thou, brother, go forward."

Then, grief-stricken at the fall of his kin, down fell Arjuna, the noble Pandava, slayer of his foes. And as the lion-hearted hero lay dying, Bhima said to the king: "In him I recall no wrong-doing; wherefore, then, is he fallen?"

Then answered Yudhishthira: "He thought to destroy his foes in one day. He failed, and he is fallen."

So the king held on his way. Then fell Bhima himself; and as he fell, he cried: "Look on me, O king! Tell me why I fall, if thou knowest!"

To him replied Yudhishthira: "Thou wert given to cursing and to gluttony, therefore art thou fallen thus." Then, regarding him not, the valiant king went on, the dog alone being his companion.

Then Indra, filling heaven and earth with sound, drew near in his car and bade Yudhishthira mount. But the king, heartbroken, answered: "My brothers lie fallen yonder; let them go with me! I care not to enter Swarga without them. The fair and delicate princess too—let her come with us!"

Said Indra: "Thy brothers are gone before thee to Swarga; there thou shalt see them, wherefore, be of good cheer."

Then said Yudhishthira further: "This dog has been my true comrade; him, too, I would have enter with me."

"This day," replied Indra, "thou gainest immortality and full delight; why trouble thyself concerning the dog? Knowest thou not that foul fiends bear away the merit of all religious acts at which a dog has been present?"

But Yudhishthira answered: "The noble cannot do that which is base. Far from me be happiness that comes with leaving a comrade."

Indra bade him consider that Swarga was no place for dogs. But Yudhishthira answered again: "It has been said, that to abandon a comrade is as bad as slaying a Brahman, and I will never abandon the dog for the sake of mere happiness."

Again Indra asked him whether he was not mad to leave his brothers and Draupadi for the sake of a mere dog.

But Yudhishthira replied: "They are dead; and I cannot bring them to life. Also, I hold that the maltreatment of one who has sought protection, the slaying of a woman, the robbing of a Brahman, and the lifting up of one's hand against a friend, are no whit worse than throwing over a faithful comrade."

On this, the dog was transformed into the god Dharma himself, who praised Yudhishthira with comfortable words, saying—

"Yudhishthira, true son of mine, I tried thee of old in the Dwaita Forest, and thou stoodest when thy brethren failed. Thou hast refused the heavenly car rather than abandon the dog that followed thee faithfully. Know, therefore, that thy peer is not to be found in all Swarga, and thou shalt go thither in thine own body, to surpassing bliss."

Then Dharma and Indra, with gods Maruts and Rishis, made Yudhishthira ascend the car, and he mounted aloft with dazzling splendour. Narada the wise and all the royal sages hailed him with praise and benediction as he came. Hearing them, and having made salutation, Yudhishthira spake thus—

"Fair or foul be the abode of my brothers, it alone do I seek, and no other."

The King of gods answered mildly: "Dwell here happily, great monarch; why consider earthly ties? Thou hast gained supreme perfection, beyond all other men; hereunto thy brethren have not attained."

But Yudhishthira answered as before: "Without them I may not live here, O Destroyer of demons. Where my brothers are, and Draupadi the virtuous, best of women, thither would I go."

Then, on going up to the heights of Swarga, he beheld Duryodhana, seated on a throne, splendid as the sun, surrounded by gods and saints. Seeing him thus enthroned, Yudhishthira turned in haste and said—

"I desire no heaven along with Duryodhana, at whose hands we have suffered such wrong; where my brothers are, thither would I go."

"Nay," said Narada, smiling, "in Swarga all enmity comes to an end. Duryodhana, having given his life in battle, as is the duty of a Kshatriya, has gained these happy realms deservedly. Think not of what was caused by the dice, nor of Draupadi's wrongs, nor of all else that befell you at your kinsmen's hands in battle or elsewhere. Come, join hands with royal Duryodhana! This is Swarga, where all strife is unknown."

But Yudhishthira asked steadfastly for his brothers, and said, "If these realms of bliss are the portion of Duryodhana the unrighteous, through whose doings earth and all its denizens were vexed, and we ourselves blasted with misery, then would I fain see the abode of my brethren, the high-souled and true. Nor do I behold here great-hearted Karna, Dhrishtadyumna, Satyaki, and the rest—where are they? Those lion-hearted, world-conquering warriors—I see them not. If they are here, well indeed! If not, I will never dwell apart from my brothers or from Karna, with whose aid we might resist even Indra himself. What have I to do with Swarga, reft of my brothers? Where they are, there is my Swarga; this is no heaven for me."

The gods then suffered him go seek his brethren's abode, and sent a celestial messenger to guide him.

Dark and difficult was the road these two followed; o'erhung with gloom, and thick with a mire of gore and putrid carcases; swarming with flies, and beset by goblins. Bones lay around; worms crawled everywhere; the air was alive with burnings. Iron-beaked crows and vultures, and huge goblins, with beaks like needles, foul with blood, infested the way. Deeply brooded the upright king as he trod this doleful road, through the horrid stench. He beheld the dread river of boiling water, and the forest of

"Dark and difficult was the Road"

which the leaves are sword-blades sharp as razors; the plains of burning sand, the jars of boiling oil, the lofty Salmali with its sharp thorns, and the torments of evil-doers.

Gazing on this horrid road, Yudhishthira asked his guide, saying, "Tell me, I pray, what road is this, and where are my brethren?"

To him replied the guide, "I was bidden by the Immortals to conduct thee hither; but if thou art weary, thou mayest return."

Then Yudhishthira, dizzy with the stench, set his heart on return. But as he turned, o'erwhelmed with misery and sorrow, he heard woeful voices accosting him thus:—

"Ho, noble Pandava, son of Dharma, abide with us but a moment, for pity's sake! Comfort came to us from the pleasant breeze that heralded thy coming. Seeing thee, we shall gain enduring comfort. If thou abidest with us even for a moment, our torments will not destroy us."

"Ah, woe the day!" cried King Yudhishthira, hearing these dismal voices all around; and, in compassion, he stopped. Again and again came those sounds of woe, but he recognised them not, and he asked—

"Who are ye, and wherefore bide ye here?"

From one side and another came the answer: "I am Karna—I, Bhima—I, Arjuna—we are Nakula and Sahadeva—I am Draupadi," and so forth.

"How now?" said Yudhishthira. "What deed of shame has been wrought by these great-hearted ones that they must dwell in this foul and awful abode? In all their virtuous lives I recall no offence. And what has Duryodhana done that he, with his friends, should dwell in bliss? Through whose fault are these heroic souls, instructed in all righteousness, ever set on following truth, gone to hell? Do I dream or wake? Am I conscious or unconscious? Ah, that it might be some wandering of my wits, some distemper of my mind!"

Thus musing, King Yudhishthira, his senses distraught with the pangs of sorrow, brake forth into hot anger, and railed at the gods and at Dharma himself. Then he said to his guide, "Get thee gone to them that sent thee. For myself, I shall never go thither, but here I stay; for through my presence my brothers find comfort."

Thus addressed, the messenger returned to the presence of the gods, and told them of King Yudhishthira's resolve, even according to his words.

Then, when the good king had stood but an instant, the gods, led by Indra, drew near, and Dharma in bodily form approached. On the coming of these bright ones, the darkness vanished, and no more were seen those torments of evil-doers. The River Vaitarni, with the lofty Salmali, the iron jars and towering crags, disappeared. A fair breeze, flinging fragrance far and wide, blew freshly, and Vasus and Maruts, saints and sages, approached with Indra the spot where the glorious son of Dharma stood. Then Indra addressed Yudhishthira with words of comfort:

"Stout-hearted Yudhishthira," he said, "the gods are well pleased with thee. Come, lion-hearted, thy work is done! Perfection and immortality are thine, sorrow is past. For, hearken! the sight of hell is expedient for every king. Moreover, as by a trick thou didst confound Drona concerning his son, so by a trick thou hast had this vision of hell, and by a trick have Bhima, Arjuna, and the others appeared to be in hell. Now they are freed from all sin; likewise thy friends slain in battle. Thou wilt see Karna, too, that prince of warriors, for whom thou mournest, resting in his place, bright as the sun. Away, then, with sorrow and heartache; and, after this short taste of anguish, enjoy in my presence the fruit of all thy labours. Bathe here in the heavenly Ganges, and leave thy earthly being behind, free from toil and strife for ever."

While the king of gods thus spake to Yudhishthira, Dharma in bodily presence addressed his son:

"Hail, wise king! Well pleased am I with thee, dear son! By loyalty to me, truthfulness, and self-control, thou hast stood my three-fold test unmoved. First I tried thee in the Dwaita forest, in the matter of the firewood; a second time, in the form of the dog, I tried thy loyalty; and now the third time, as to thy willingness to abide with thy brethren. Now thou art free from all stain, nor have thy brothers any portion in hell. This has been nought but illusion, put forth by the king of gods."

Thus addressed, Yudhishthira went with Dharma and the other dwellers on high; and having plunged in the river of the gods, he left his human body and took on a divine form. Then, hymned by great sages, he arose and went to the place where the lion-hearted Pandavas and the sons of Dhritarashtra alike abode, each in his portion, for ever free from sorrow, in the company of the Immortals.

APPENDIX

Appendix

LIST OF HINDU GODS MENTIONED IN THESE TALES

Agni . . . god of Fire.

Aswins . . two twin deities, like the Greek Castor and Pollux

Brahma. . the Creator. He is the first of a triad or trinity, the other two being Vishnu and Siva.

Dharma . Duty or Righteousness, sometimes personified as a god.

Indra . . god of Thunder. His heaven is called Swarga.

Krishna . one of the Incarnations of Vishnu, the eighth in number, coming after Rama. Very popular in recent times.

Kuvera. . god of Wealth, with a special heaven called Kailasa.

Lakshmi . the wife of Vishnu, goddess of Happiness and Beauty.

Mahadeva. "the great god": a name of Siva.

Rama . . the seventh Incarnation of Vishnu. See the *Ramayana.*

Saraswati. wife of Brahma, goddess of learning.

Sesha . . the great Serpent, on which the world rests.

Siva. . . the third of the Hindu Triad. He is called the Destroyer, and is worshipped in many wild and shocking ways. He is particularly the god of religious mendicants and ascetics.

Surya . . the Sun-god.

Varuna. . god of the Sky.

Vayu. . god of the Wind.

Vishnu. . the second of the Hindu Triad. He is called the Preserver, and is said to have ten Incarnations, of which nine are past and one is yet to come. Rama was the seventh, and Krishna the eighth.

Yama . . the god of Death and departed spirits.

LIST OF VARIOUS SUPERHUMAN BEINGS

DAITYAS AND DANAVAS .	Titans, generally hostile to the gods.
GANDHARVAS .	the choristers of Indra's heaven, though the name is given also to beings dwelling elsewhere.
GARUDA . .	a kind of celestial bird, upon which Vishnu rode, constantly at war with the Serpents.
MARUTS . .	storm-gods.
NAGAS . . .	beings of a form half human, half snake-like, dwelling in Pàtala, the Under-world—a place distinct from Hades and Hell.
RAKSHASAS .	fiends of a thoroughly malignant nature. Their most famous abode was Lanka, or Ceylon, where they lived under Ravana, their king.
RISHIS. . .	divine Sages, raised to that position by holy lives on earth. They had extraordinary powers, often nearly equal to those of the gods themselves. The name of the Rishi Narada occurs frequently in these tales; Vasishtha, Viswamitra, Markandeya, and Agastya are also mentioned.
VASUS . . .	attendants upon Indra, chiefly connected with natural phenomena.
VEDAS . . .	the most ancient Scriptures of the Hindus.
VRIHASPATI .	the ruler of the planet Jupiter.
YAKSHAS . .	attendants on Kuvera; usually harmless in character.

THE FOUR CASTES

BRAHMANAS commonly called Brahmans, the priests of the Hindus.

KSHATRIYAS warriors and kings.

VAISYAS . whose business was agriculture.

SUDRAS . who were originally slaves, or given to employments inferior to those of the first three castes.

Of these, the first three are sharply separated from the Sudras, who alone are not allowed to wear what is called the sacred thread. Kshatriyas and Vaisyas are not so common as in ancient India; on the other hand, the Sudra caste is divided up into all kinds of divisions, the highest of which are considered very respectable—some, indeed, hold themselves almost equal to Brahmans. Members of one caste are not allowed to marry those of another, and this rule applies to the minor divisions of each caste as well. Also the Brahmans consider themselves so holy that they will not touch food or drink offered to them by some of the lower castes; in fact, a Brahman who did so would be considered to have committed a dreadful crime, and would be severely punished by the society of his caste.

SOME FAMOUS HINDU SCRIPTURES

VEDAS . . . These are the most ancient, and are supposed to be the groundwork of all truly Hindu religion. They are regarded with the deepest respect, but the great mass of the people know absolutely nothing of their contents.

RAMAYANA . . The Tale of Rama. An immense poem, describing the incarnation of Vishnu as Rama. The story in this book is drawn from it.

MAHABHARATA. A still longer poem—no less than 210,000 lines in length—of which the Tale of the Pandava Brethren, as related in this book, is the subject.

PURANAS . . Religious poems of a very mixed character, from which the real religion of the modern Hindu is drawn. Some of the stories in this book are taken from the Puranas.

PRONUNCIATION OF NAMES

To readers unfamiliar with Indian names, a few simple hints about pronunciation may be useful. In the index long vowels will be indicated by a straight mark, and an accent will generally be found on one syllable or another.

- *a* is not to be pronounced like the ordinary short *a* in English, but like our *u* in *but*, or like the dull sound of the final syllable in such words as *nation*, *finger*, *metal*.
- *ā* is broad, as in *bar*, *half*.
- *i* as in French or German, like English *e*; ī, similar, but rather longer.
- *o* always long, as in *bore*.
- *u* as in German, or *u* in English *full*; *ū*, rather longer.
- *e* like *a* in *spare*.
- *ai* like *i* in *rise*.
- *au* like *ou* in *hound*.
- *ph*, *th* in these the *h* does not combine with the other letter, as in English, but should be kept separate, as in *up-hill*, *boat-hook*.

Otherwise, for practical purposes, the consonants may be pronounced as in English. There are several points of difference, but they are hardly of importance in such a book as this. Readers accurately acquainted with the spelling of Indian names will easily understand that it is undesirable here to lay much stress upon any but the most salient points.

INDEX

Index

A hyphen is occasionally introduced to mark an important syllabic division.